"This message needs to be our greatest priority: staying close to the Father.
Everything we need in life comes from our connection with Him. The way Jesus lived and moved came out of relationship. Diane writes with great clarity on the significance and rewards of close proximity to God's heart. Whether your heart is distant, or you feel the pull to draw nearer, this book will be your guide."

- Tim Spirk
Senior Associate Pastor at Christ Community Church, Camp Hill

"We live in a time where the power and presence of God is needed more than ever. It seems as though the church has lain dormant and immobilized. *CLOSER* is a practical how-to guide for both new and old Christians. Diane Burke has been a member of Global Awakening's Network for almost fifteen years, and it has been a joy to get to know her the past few years as I've served as the Director of the Network. In this book, she explains how to have a powerful, Holy Spirit filled life through a personal relationship with Him. Her book contains often-forgotten teachings about the place of the Word of God, intercession, and fasting, while removing so much of the religiosity commonly connected to these topics. So, no matter where you are in your walk with Jesus, if you want to know Him more, experience revival, and see His power overflow out of your life, I highly recommend taking the time to read this book."

- Dr. Michael Van't Hul
Director of Global Awakening

"I have had the privilege of knowing Diane for years now and can testify that the message in this book is something that she truly lives daily. As a leader and someone who cares deeply for the health of Christ's church, this book is a clarion call to the Body of Christ to draw closer to Jesus during this seemingly chaotic time of upheaval in our country. This book is an invitation to all in His church, including leaders, to come back to our first love, to draw near to our Bridegroom, and prioritize time in His presence, knowing Him once again. Diane's message is clear: knowing Jesus allows us to successfully represent Him well in every sphere of life and ministry while avoiding the pitfalls that can easily ensnare. Let us heed this timely and prophetic call, and once again, draw near to Jesus."

- Peter Neuberger
President and Founder of Kashabba Tribe Ministries

CLOSER

WAYS TO DRAW AND STAY NEAR TO GOD

DIANE BURKE

Copyright © 2025 by Diane Burke

All rights reserved. This book or any portion thereof may not be reproduced or used in any manner without the express written permission of Diane Burke Ministries, Inc. except for the use of brief quotations in a book review.

Printed in the United States of America.

ISBN: 978-1-7367523-1-9

"Scripture taken from the NEW AMERICAN STANDARD BIBLE, Copyright © 1960, 1962, 1963, 1968. 1971, 1972, 1973, 1975, 1977, 1995 by The Lockman Foundation. Used by permission. www.Lockman.org"

Dedication

I dedicate this book to my husband, children, and grandchildren. Intimacy and closeness with God are my priority, and I pray it is yours as well. Your love and encouragement continue to bless me, and I thank God for you. May God's favor surround you all the days of your lives.

Acknowledgements

Thank you, Caitlin, for your unwavering support and encouragement. The process from a book idea to print is a long one with many adjustments along the way. You have been patient, kind, inspiring, and very helpful. As we cross the finish line, it is time to trust God for the next phase of encouraging readers to draw closer to Him.

Contents

Introduction	1
1. Why Closeness Matters	5
2. The Word's Impact	13
3. Obedience	25
4. Let Your Heart Sing	37
5. Compartmentalization	51
6. Community	61
7. Fasting	69
8. Navigate Disappointment	79
9. Receive and Release Love	91
10. Hear God's Heart	103
11. Withstand Culture	115
12. Advance the Kingdom	123
13. Represent Jesus	131
14. Holy Spirit Operations	143
15. Closer	153
Salvation	159
Notes	161
About the Author	162

Introduction

As a watchwoman in the body of Christ, I have observed Christian leaders caught in the grips of sin, falling by the wayside. What is happening to those with powerful platforms? Where does the downward spiral start? Why have leaders fallen prey to the enemy rather than standing firm in the faith, resisting temptation? Is there any explanation?

Why are we losing our young adults after they grow up in godly homes? What happens when they go to college and now must live off their own faith? Why are our young people seeking other forms of fulfilment?

Our world has strayed from godly values and morals to an anything-goes mentality. It wants us to tolerate, accept, and welcome whatever people feel like doing, being, or becoming. Challenges face our society as we are witnessing destructive tendencies. People have no regard for Jesus and His call to follow Him.

When the Lord first spoke to me about this book, I replied that others were more qualified to write it. Oftentimes, however, the Lord takes authors through the very thing which they end up writing about. Jesus continues to draw me closer, even after years of following Him. My goal is loving God through hardship as well as through the good times, with nothing severing my connection.

My desire is to help people find ways to become so close to the Lord, that no amount of shaking from the world—no amount of peer pressure, sinful temptation, nor discouragement—will steal their hope and lead them down a wayward path. "I have set the Lord continually before me, because He is at my right hand, I will not be shaken," (Psalm 16:8).

Closeness with God is not only about standing firm. The closer we become, the more we experience His goodness in every area of life. Surrendering all to Him results in His grace no matter what we are doing. I am no longer interested in living for myself, asking God to bless my endeavors. My quest continues to be representing Jesus, whether I am preaching on the mission field, playing with grandkids or cleaning the house.

CHAPTER 1

Why Closeness Matters

Our daughter and her husband live several states away, and they have four sons. We can call our grandsons on the phone. We can make video calls. We can even visit and stay in a nearby hotel. Of all the ways to communicate, the most satisfying is when we visit and stay in their home, experiencing life together. From playing games, watching their sports, and walking the dogs, to bedtime stories and prayers, our connections grow stronger being together.

I believe God desires this type of relationship with us—where we live life together in partnership, making decisions, dreaming, exploring ideas, working, and playing. He is the author of abundant life, and His written word is our lifestyle manual. Drawing closer to Him is a continuous journey, not only to withstand the attacks of the enemy, but to live in this divine union for which God created us. Jesus expresses His immense love for us in John 15:9: "Just as the Father has loved me, I have also loved you. Abide in My love."

We have a choice: to live in agreement with the kingdom of light or the kingdom of darkness. Who are we partnered with? Are the decisions that we make and live by in alignment with the word of God? Are they decisions in agreement with the enemy? Or are they made from selfish desires?

There are blatant evil forces in every sphere of society trying to persuade unsuspecting victims. If you don't know what you believe, others will tell you. The anger and mean spiritedness go beyond rationale. Our nation is under spiritual attack, and we must be on the alert.

The family unit is breaking away from God's design. We no longer have one-man and one-woman marriages. Same-sex marriage is becoming more common. Fathers are absent and single moms are heavily laden with responsibilities. "Children from fatherless homes are more likely to be poor, become involved in drug and alcohol abuse, drop out of school, and suffer from health and emotional problems. Boys are more likely to become involved in crime, and girls are more likely to become pregnant as teens."[1]

"And just as they did not see fit to acknowledge God any longer, God gave them over to a depraved mind, to do those things which are not proper, being filled with all unrighteousness, wickedness, greed, evil; full of envy, murder, strife, deceit, malice; they are gossips, slanderers, haters of God, insolent, arrogant, boastful, inventors of evil, disobedient to parents, without understanding, untrustworthy, unloving, unmerciful..."

Romans 1:28-31

As people choose to disregard God and His ways, we see the consequences of their actions. There is no godly wisdom in the soul of the one making his or her own decisions. Evil spirits in our atmosphere are colluding with those who are lost. Believers who have one foot in the world and one foot in the kingdom are also affected by the powers of evil. This is not the time to wonder which kingdom you belong to. As Joshua tells the Israelites in Joshua 24:15, "...choose for yourselves this day whom you will serve, ...but as for me and my house, we will serve the Lord."

Our spiritual journey is no different than other passions we pursue. The more attention we give anything, the more our affection increases towards it. We spend time doing what attracts us. This works both positively and negatively. We can bear good fruit pursuing positive, healthy interests just as bad fruit can come from negative, sinful activity.

We have one hundred sixty-eight hours per week. Navigating how we spend our time is ongoing as the seasons of life change. While our children are young, they take up lots of time. Jobs may require overtime or finishing work at home. Work, family, chores, exercise, entertainment, sports: a vast number of tasks compete for our attention. On any given day, at any given time, I have several things I could be doing. Our kids are grown, my husband is retired, so the options are many.

I ask for the Lord's help to navigate my time. For me, time spent with God in the morning is a priority. I can get His perspective on my day and prepare myself spiritually for what lies ahead. For others, night may be better. I recall when my kids were little, and I decided to wake up in the middle of the night and spend one hour with the Lord from 2:00 a.m. to 3:00 a.m. Let's just say, that did not work even one night. I ended that idea and started praying in bed before falling asleep. It was the only way. I now spend early morning with Him, and at bedtime I give Him thanks for what happened in the day.

I have three adult children who are avid fitness fans. The gym is a brilliant analogy for how time spent produces results. People understand that exercise builds muscle while encouraging better health and longevity of life. Likewise, in our Christian journey, time spent with the Lord in the secret place equates to an intimate personal relationship. The strengthening of our spirit man is much like the strengthening of our core in the fitness world—one is natural, and one is spiritual.

Just like our core muscles determine our posture, our spirit man determines our posture in how we relate to people and circumstances.

At first, it may seem like work to spend extra time with the Lord. In fact, you may have no interest in doing such a thing; however, once the Holy Spirit begins to meet you, it soon becomes a desire and delight. Your affection towards the Lord will increase and your spiritual muscles will grow. The closer we get to the Lord, the stronger our love relationship becomes

Throughout the remainder of this book, we will explore ways to grow closer to God and discuss why this relationship is important. First and foremost, the Lord desires a close, personal relationship with us because He loves us. Second, He wants to strengthen us in these days of adversity so we can shine His light and dispel darkness. Third, we are called to do the works that Jesus did, representing Christ and inviting people to know Him. The closer we are to our Heavenly Father the more others will sense His presence around us and be drawn to Him.

Chapter Nuggets

- We have a choice to live in agreement with the kingdom of light or the kingdom of darkness.
- We choose how we spend our time.
- It is with intentionality that we decide how to incorporate daily quiet time into our schedule.
- What begins as a decision of discipline, becomes a desire and delight.
- Our spiritual muscle is needed to strengthen us against attack and abide in His love.
- The strengthening of our spirit man is much like increasing our core muscles in fitness training.
- We are called to represent Christ and invite people to know Him.

CLOSER

CHAPTER 2

The Word's Impact

One morning I woke up and to my dismay, I had five enlarged knuckles on my left hand! At first, I was scared, recalling my mother complaining of arthritis at various times in her later years. I assumed this had something to do with arthritis. I began to use my "word" arsenal, the scriptures that speak of healing. Faith rose up as I declared my healing by the stripes of Jesus, and by day's end my hand returned to normal. God is good! No more issues.

The Word of God is our manual for living a kingdom lifestyle. The Bible has sixty-six books with forty-four authors, all inspired by the Holy Spirit. It reveals who God is, why Jesus came to earth, and the person of the Holy Spirit. The more we know the word of God, the more we know His ways.

> "All scripture is inspired by God and profitable for teaching, for reproof, for correction, for training in righteousness; so that the man of God may be adequate, equipped for every good work."
> 2 Timothy 3:16-17

The Bible trains us to become disciples of Jesus Christ. It is meant to be read interactively. The scriptures are transformational agents that go deep into our hearts and bring divine alignment with God and His kingdom. The ways of the world are contrary to God's ways. Without His manual, it would be difficult to understand God's will.

Forgiveness is a good example. In Matthew 18:21b-22, Peter asks Jesus, "'Lord, how often shall my brother sin against me and I forgive Him? Up to seven times?' Jesus said to him, 'I do not say to you, up to seven times, but up to seventy times seven.'" Jesus tells us to forgive for our personal freedom, and because unforgiveness disconnects us from Him. Without the word of God, we would not know that Jesus tells us to forgive others as Christ has forgiven us.

"Be kind to one another, tender-hearted, forgiving each other, just as God in Christ also has forgiven you."

Ephesians. 4:32

Over the past couple years with the division in America, I have needed to forgive people I don't even know. Forgiveness is necessary in every area of life including family relationships, friendships, jobs, church, social media, and more. Unforgiveness is sin and will create distance in our relationship with the Lord.

The Bible teaches us to live with steadfast faith in God. Hebrews 10:38a declares, "Now the just shall live by faith...". What is faith? The Bible tells us that, "...faith is the substance of things hoped for, the evidence of things not seen," (Hebrews 11:1b NKJV).

Faith speaks what God says in His word. God's word is the power of His kingdom released into the earth. As Jesus teaches us to pray in Matthew 6:10, "Your kingdom come, Your will be done on earth as it is in heaven." Whether releasing prophecy, healing, or deliverance, God's power is activated by speaking His word in faith. How quickly we see results varies, but faith is released when we pray.

Our faith is developed through hearing the word of God and speaking it. As we read through the Bible, believing God's word and applying it, we see results. Every time Jesus was tempted by the devil in the wilderness, He used the written word to combat the enemy and gain victory.

After Jesus' baptism, the Holy Spirit led Him into the wilderness. When Jesus had fasted forty days, the devil tried to tempt Him to turn a stone into bread. Jesus said, "It is written, man shall not live on bread alone..." He was then led to where the devil showed Him all the kingdoms of the world, and was told, "All these things I will give You, if You fall down and worship me," (Matthew 4:9b). Jesus answered, "It is written, you shall worship the Lord your God and serve Him only." Finally, the devil led Him to the pinnacle in Jerusalem and told Jesus to throw Himself down, for angels will protect Him. ' Jesus responded a third time, "It is said, 'you shall not put the Lord your God to the test.'" The devil left Him.

The Word's Impact

(Paraphrased from Matthew 4:1-10). The word of God is the authority we have through Christ to overcome the power of the enemy.

God's word is like manna, it feeds us. Drawing closer to Him will involve giving Him more time to communicate through His word. There are multiple levels of revelation and understanding, and the moment we think we know it all, the Holy Spirit will show us a deeper truth. He will highlight verses, chapters, or entire books for us to read and or study.

When we receive Jesus, our thought life needs an overhaul. Prior to salvation, our thoughts were worldly and consumed with self. Now that we have exchanged our life for God's, we need to think like Him. God's word will show us the mind of Christ so we can adapt our thinking to His.

"And do not be conformed to this world, but be transformed by the renewing of your mind, so that you may prove what the will of God is, that which is good and acceptable and perfect."

Romans 12:2

Thoughts come before words. What we mediate on ends up revealing itself through the things we say. Proverbs 18:21 says, "Death and life are in the power of the tongue, and those who love it will eat its fruit." This is a radical verse, true in all aspects. Our words activate kingdoms. Unless we become aware of what we are thinking and saying, and realize that negative words can curse and harm, we will not change what we say.

"...for whatever a man sows, this he will also reap. For the one who sows to his own flesh will from the flesh reap corruption, but the one who sows to the Spirit will from the Spirit reap eternal life." Galatians 6:7-8.

The principle of sowing and reaping applies to believers and non-believers. The words that we sow will produce positive or negative results. Curse words are words that quench the spirit, diminish, belittle, cut down, depress, and more. Parents that speak negatively to their children will affect their identity. Our identity is impacted by the words spoken to us, either encouraging or discouraging.

Positive, life-giving words can build, promote great self-esteem, and make for a healthy identity.

The Word's Impact

Thinking of our new granddaughter, who gets lots of wonderful accolades and smiles from ear to ear, she knows she's loved. It is so important that we think about what we speak and how our words affect ourselves and others.

> "Let no unwholesome word proceed from your mouth, but only such a word as is good for edification according to the need of the moment, so that it will give grace to those that hear."
>
> Ephesians 4:29

People can recall negative words from their childhood that they have believed from authority figures. Words bear fruit, good or bad. The renewing of our minds is to fill our hearts with the truth of God's word, removing worldly, selfish, and destructive thoughts. Thoughts become words and thereby release blessing or cursing. Let us be a people that blesses.

As we meditate on scripture, renewing our mind, the word of God moves from head knowledge to heart knowledge. His words take root in our hearts and help us respond in a godly manner to people and circumstances. As our minds begin to think like Christ, our words will align with His, and our actions will bring God glory.

The word of God is the expressed will of God. The more time we spend reading it—the more we apply it to our lives—the more our lives will take on the attributes of Christ. This process develops our love relationship with the Lord and draws us closer to Him. Jesus came that we may have His new life, beginning the day of our salvation.

The scriptures carry the breath of God. The words on each page of the Bible have power. Here are a few verses to address the situations we face in life:

- "Be anxious for nothing but in everything by prayer and supplication with Thanksgiving, let your requests be made known to God. And the peace of God which surpasses all understanding, will guard your hearts and minds in Christ Jesus." Philippians 4:6-7
- "For God hath not given us the spirit of fear; but of power, and of love, and of a sound mind." 2 Timothy 1:7 KJ

- "And my God will supply all your needs according to His riches in glory in Christ Jesus." Philippians 4:19
- "For nothing will be impossible with God." Luke 1:37
- "Bless the Lord, O my soul, and forget none of His benefits, who pardons all your iniquities, who heals all your diseases." Psalm 103:2-3
- "...Have faith in God, truly I say to you, whoever says to this mountain, 'Be taken up and cast into the sea,' and does not doubt in his heart, but believes that what he says is going to happen, it will be granted him." Mark 11:22-23
- "I can do all things through Him who strengthens me." Philippians 4:13
- "The Lord is my rock, and my fortress, and my deliverer..." Psalm 18:2a
- "My help comes from the Lord, who made heaven and earth." Ps. 121:2

There are over thirty-one thousand verses in the Bible. My sampling of nine on this page is for illustration. We can look up verses that address our needs. As we declare God's word into our need, we can expect a victorious result.

In Genesis chapter one, God spoke into existence the entirety of creation and the existence of man. "Then God said, 'Let there be light,' and there was light," (Genesis 1:3). Jesus spoke, and miracles occurred. "...He cried out with a loud voice, 'Lazarus come forth!'" after Lazarus was dead for four days (John 11:43). Even our salvation comes with making a confession: In Romans 10:9, we're told, "if you confess with your mouth Jesus as Lord and believe in your heart that God raised Him from the dead, you will be saved..." Our words spoken in faith carry power.

Prayer groups are rising throughout America and across the face of the earth. Decrees are being made to release Heaven on earth. We are living in times of uncertainty, chaos, and darkness. How do we respond? We speak God's word. Jeremiah 1:12b says, "...I am watching over my word to perform it."

How does God's word draw us closer to Him? The book of Psalms is a great book to find verses of adoration, praise, and worship for our Lord. It also shows us effective ways to express our love. I have found the following help draw me closer to the Lord:

> Praise: Celebrating what God has done.
>
> Worship: Celebrating who God is.
>
> Thanksgiving: Thanking Him for the good I see every day.
>
> Adoration: Telling God how amazing He is and how much I love Him.

It is fascinating how God speaks to us through His written word. You and I can find situations in the Bible that mirror what we are experiencing in life and receive hope. God's word is essential to our growth, our understanding and knowledge in spiritual matters, while also releasing power as we speak it.

Chapter Nuggets

- The word of God is our manual for kingdom living.
- Faith is developed through God's word.
- The more we know the word of God, the more we know His ways.
- The word of God defeats the enemy.
- Words activate blessing or cursing.
- Every situation we face has corresponding scriptures.
- God's word is essential to our growth, our understanding and knowledge in spiritual matters.

CHAPTER 3

Obedience

The Lord continues to stretch my faith regarding finances. He typically asks me to sow a financial seed for the ministry provision I need. Last year, He asked me to give into our church's first fruits offering, trusting Him to provide the money I needed for a later trip to Rwanda, Africa. He then gave me an idea to ask people for a donation of twenty-five dollars for this trip of thirty-six hundred. I obeyed.

I was surprised by the abundant provision. After travel costs were covered, I had funds to give out fifty Bibles to new believers, sow into local ministries there, give to the missionary leading the trip, give away twenty teaching books, donate my own books, bless women with lollipops, and gift soccer balls to kids.

Let us talk about obedience from a heavenly perspective. Through our actions, we are obeying *something*. We either follow the ways of our flesh, the ways of the enemy, or the ways of the Lord. Obeying God becomes our desire as we pursue relationship with Him and cultivate our Kingdom mindset.

We can't talk about obedience until we define sin. Sin is "missing the mark." Picture an archery target. Anything outside the bullseye is sin including missing the target completely. No one is perfect, except Jesus. The rest of us sin. It could be in our thought life, words, or actions. Jesus died and rose from the dead, conquering the power of sin. He has given us His authority over temptations and sin's power. If we fall short, our sin is forgiven as we confess unto Him.

"If we confess our sins, He is faithful and just to forgive us our sins and to cleanse us from all unrighteousness."

1 John 1:9

Obedience

Right from the very beginning in Genesis, when God spoke the world into creation, He planted two trees in the garden of Eden. Man had a choice: there was the tree of knowledge of good and evil, and the tree of life. Eve was tempted by the devil to eat of the tree of good and evil—the one God told Adam not to. "When the woman saw that the tree was good for food, and that it was a delight to the eyes, and that the tree was desirable to make one wise, she took from its fruit and ate; and she gave also to her husband with her, and he ate. Then the eyes of both of them were opened, and they knew they were naked;" (Genesis 3:6-7). At the moment of disobedience, sin entered mankind.

The Israelites, led out of captivity in Egypt, failed in keeping the Ten Commandments. They did not even wait for Moses to return from the mountain where God was writing the commandments on stone tablets before they engaged in idolatry with the golden calf. The Old Testament is full of examples where disobedience is judged by God.

Thankfully, you and I are living in a superior covenant. Since Jesus showed up, we no longer sacrifice animals to atone for sin. He is the perfect sacrificial lamb that takes away the sin of the world. The beauty of this new covenant is we have the internal help of the Holy Spirit to live life in obedience to the Lord. The Old Testament law was hard to keep because it did not change the heart of man. The Israelites went astray in their hearts after being delivered from Egypt, following other gods, so the Lord did not allow them to enter the promised land. Therefore, they wandered in the wilderness for forty years.

Let's establish the Biblical definition of obedience: "To hear God's Word and act accordingly. The word translated 'obey' in the OT [Old Testament] means 'to hear' and is often so translated. In the NT [New Testament] several words describe obedience. One word means 'to hear or to listen in a state of submission.' Another NT word often translated 'obey' means 'to trust.' The person's obedient response to God's Word is a response of trust or faith. Thus, to really hear God's Word is to obey God's word..."[2]

God's word also tells us how to love God and people. It teaches how to live according to His ways, our manual for righteous living. The Bible is not a book for your bookshelf, never to be utilized. Rather, it defines His way of life for us through the divine assistance of the Holy Spirit. The Holy Spirit empowers us to live life in obedience to His word, as we come into agreement, receiving grace for every situation.

God says that following His commandments demonstrates our love for Him. "If you love Me, you will keep My commandments," (John 14:15). What are those again? They can be summarized in two directives: love God and love people. In my personal journey, the more I love God, the more I obey. The more I obey, the more I love Him. It works both ways. The key to obeying the Lord is surrendering our will, laying down our life in exchange for His. As Paul says in Galatians 2:20, "I have been crucified with Christ; and it is no longer I who live, but Christ lives in me; and the life which I now live in the flesh, I live by faith in the Son of God who loved me and gave Himself up for me."

Obedience unto the Lord results in a healthy lifestyle. He tells us:

- "The steadfast of mind You will keep in perfect peace, because he trusts in You." Isaiah 26:3
- "...whatever is true, whatever is honorable, whatever is right, whatever is pure, whatever is lovely, whatever is of good repute, if there is any excellence and if anything worthy of praise, dwell on these things." Philippians 4:8
- "Be kind to one another, tenderhearted, forgiving each other, just as God in Christ as also forgiven you. Eph. 4:32
- "Let no unwholesome word proceed from your mouth, but only such a word as is good for edification according to the need of the moment, so that it will give grace to those that hear." Ephesians 4:29
- "...casting all your anxiety on Him because He cares for you. " 1 Peter 5:7
- "...walk by the Spirit, and you will not carry out the desire of the flesh." Galatians 5:16
- "Just as the Father has loved Me, I have also loved you; Abide in My love." John 15:9
- "But seek first His kingdom and His righteousness, and all these things shall be added unto you." Matthew 6:33

- "...I came that they may have life and have it abundantly." John 10:10

God does not ask us to do anything that is to our detriment. His ways are good, healthy, and sound. He is not the author of evil and destruction. He is not trying to teach us through suffering, nor is He causing it. He is not an abusive Father. God can transform a negative situation, without having caused it. Everything that happens on earth is not the will of God. If all that took place on earth was the will of God, everyone would be saved. 2 Peter 3:9b tells us that God does not want "any to perish, but for all to come to repentance." If all that happened on the earth would be God's will, heaven on earth would be our reality.

When we face decisions—the solutions to which are not explicitly stated in the Bible—hearing God's voice allows us to obey Him and make wise choices. Choosing a career, place to live, church family, navigating finances, relationships, ministry, kids, and more: you can talk to God about every decision in life. His wisdom is there for the asking.

> "But if any of you lack wisdom. Let him ask of God, who gives to all generously and without reproach, and it will be given him."
>
> James 1:5

The closer you are to Him, the easier it is to recognize His voice. God started speaking to His people in the first book of the Bible. In Genesis 1:28 it says, "God blessed them; and God said to them, 'Be fruitful and multiply, and fill the earth, and subdue it.'" Throughout the Old Testament, God spoke primarily through prophets, kings, and priests. God would release His message to those who were called to deliver His word, and obedience from the hearers would bring about a blessing. Disobedience would result in falling away.

The Bible is full of stories of people being given an assignment and doing great exploits. Abraham hears God say he will have a son and be a father to many nations. Moses hears God say to deliver the Israelites. Noah hears God say to build an ark. Samuel hears God say to anoint David king. Job hears God speak out of a whirlwind. Elijah hears God to have a showdown with Baal. All the prophets heard God speak, then they were called to release God's word in obedience. There is a responsibility for the hearers to obey the word.

In the New Testament, the abiding presence of the Holy Spirit is within every believer, not only prophets. Everyone can hear the voice of God. We don't need to depend on the words of other believers, we can hear ourselves. Although, prophets, mentors and godly friends can help confirm if we are hearing His voice.

Navigating life with Christ is not quite as easy as the GPS in our vehicles. It would be so wonderful if we heard His voice that clearly. "Take the exit. Stay in this lane." We have mileage, the time of arrival, and after a wrong turn we hear, "Recalculating!" However, if we earnestly seek God's heart for direction, He will communicate.

Another aspect of hearing God's voice is called "conviction." While God does not force us to do anything, He does convict us for wrongdoing. Good Faith Media defines conviction as: "the way the spirit of God tugs at the heart of someone and urges confession, repentance, and rightful redirection." Conviction may come when the temptation to sin shows up. Conviction may come upon a lost person and prompt salvation. Conviction may come when we are going the wrong direction. This is our friend, as it leads us to repentance.

Obedience is a test for us all right now with our climate of chaos. Are we praying for our enemies? Are we praising rather than complaining? Are we loving rather than cursing? Are we judging in God's place? Are we angry and throwing punches instead of calling forth our nation for God's purposes to prevail? The spiritual climate is tempting for all these things, yet God's word is counterculture and obedience to Him will bring the reformation we need.

The stronger our love for the Lord is—the closer we are to His heart—the less sin is a temptation. Yes, we have habits to change, as God continues to transform us into the image of Christ. However, the closer we are to Him, the more we are aware of missing the mark, the more quickly we repent. Let us seek to partner with Jesus in every aspect of life and live from His grace. May we live from faith and grace, in obedience, bringing Him glory in all we do.

Chapter Nuggets

- Biblical obedience means to hear God's word and act accordingly.
- Closeness to God increases your desire to obey.
- The key to obeying is surrendering your will.
- God does not ask us to do anything to our detriment.
- Everyone can hear God's voice.
- Conviction is the inner prompting of the Holy Spirit unto salvation, repentance, or "rightful redirection."
- The closer we are to God's heart the less sin is a temptation.

CLOSER

CHAPTER 4

Let Your Heart Sing

I sometimes find myself in worship services in other countries where I do not know the language, or the melody. I choose to worship anyway. Even if I don't know the words, I understand that we can enter the presence of God many ways. With arms raised, I may sing in the Spirit, picture myself with Jesus, or make up my own song. God loves all types of music, even if it is off key. It is the attitude of our heart that attracts Him.

Worship is an expression of devotion and adoration unto the Lord. We worship because we honor who He is. He is worthy, He is Holy, He is our Redeemer and Friend. There is no one more supreme. He is above all, glorious and majestic. Webster's New World College Dictionary-defines worship as "extreme devotion, intense love, or admiration of any kind."

The Biblical definition of worship, understanding the Greek and Hebrew: "Worship involves intimacy and submission, yielding to the Lord. Many of the Greek and Hebrew words used in the Bible show physical expressions and acts, like laying facedown, prostrated before the Lord. They show service and adoration. True worship is complete submission of us before Him and involves more than verbal worship. Songs alone are not worship. True Biblical worship involves a heart attitude and being yielded."[3]

The world offers many counterfeit objects of worship: money, positions of power, materialism, cars, movie stars, musicians, professional athletes, and so on. The enemy likes to deceive us, taking our devotion away from the Lord. Worshipping the Lord keeps our relationship with Him steadfast and helps it grow even stronger. It keeps our heart in the right place. This is a practice which enriches our love and draws us closer to Him.

We don't worship God because our life is as smooth as silk. We don't worship Him because we have no problems, adversities, or trials. The world is full of trouble. We worship because we are elevating Jesus above every difficulty, trusting His abiding presence to lead us through the fire and sustain us. We worship because no matter what, He is worthy, and He is God. We worship the very One who knows us, formed us, loves us, and sent His Son to die for us.

The book of Psalms is great for worship. David wrote many songs that share his feelings of distress, only to turn around and honor God:

"How long, O Lord? Will You forget me forever? How long will You hide your face from me? How long shall I take counsel in my soul, having sorrow in my heart, all the day? How long will my enemy be exalted over me?

Consider and answer me, O Lord my God. Enlighten my eyes, or I will sleep the sleep of death, and my enemy will say, 'I have overcome him.' And my adversaries will rejoice when I am shaken.

But, I have trusted in Your lovingkindness; my heart shall rejoice in Your salvation. I will sing to the Lord because He has dealt bountifully with me."

Psalm 13:1-6

Throughout the book of Psalms, praise is mentioned well over one hundred times. David was continually praising God after he poured out his woes. Praise celebrates the name of Jesus above every circumstance and issue. It also exhibits joy, and joy is a strength (Nehemiah 8:10). When we praise through trials, we are not celebrating the difficulty; we are glorifying the One who leads us through victoriously. While our flesh wants to complain, our spirit is ready to praise the One who can deliver us. We can praise before the answer or outcome, for it activates God's supernatural power into our trouble. Praise rises above our trials and gives thanks to the faithful One who is always present with us, ready to defend, redeem, fortify, and advance.

The Bible is full of examples of praise. Shouts of praise filled the air as Moses led tens of thousands of people out of the clutches of bondage in Egypt. After four hundred years of slavery, there was much dancing in the streets. The Egyptians were so afraid of God at this point that they gave away their silver and gold to the former slaves.

In another instance, David was dancing with all his might as he brought the ark of the covenant into the city of David. His praise and dancing were so euphoric that his wife, Michal, despised him. She became barren because of her disparaging attitude watching David dance before the Lord.

A favorite Bible story of mine on praise is found in Acts 16:16-30. Paul and Silas were traveling, preaching. They freed a slave girl from an evil spirit that had provided income for her masters. Her masters were furious. Seeing their profit was gone, they had Paul and Silas disrobed, beaten with rods, and thrown in jail.

About midnight, the two were praying and singing hymns of praise to God. All the prisoners were listening. Suddenly, there came a great earthquake. The prison doors were shaken and immediately they were all opened. The prison guard was going to kill himself, thinking the prisoners had escaped and harsh punishment awaited him. When Paul stepped up and said, "Do not harm yourself, we are all here!" The prison guard fell down in front of Paul and asked, "What must I do to be saved?"

In the middle of beatings and imprisonment, rather than question God, "Why did this happen to us?" Paul and Silas chose to pray and praise. Right there in persecution, they chose to exalt God.

Praise celebrates what God has done. It is a weapon that activates Heaven. As we lift our gaze from the trouble to our Defender and Deliverer, we are strengthened. Praise is more than something reserved for Sunday morning at church. No matter what the world is doing, we always have something to celebrate.

Praise is also a way to celebrate testimonies. What wonderful things has God done for you? Our salvation is a praiseworthy testimony. I received Jesus in my early teen years. I owned a horse and while riding through the woods, I had conversations with the Lord. I knew in my heart He was real. Although my family went to a Lutheran church, that was not where I met Jesus. Rather, receiving salvation took place right in my bedroom.

Since then, I am awed by the amazing things God does for me, my family, and in my ministry. I believe the biggest praise for me after salvation is the fact that fifty plus years after choosing Jesus, I am still in love and more passionate for God than ever.

"Praise the Lord! Praise God in His sanctuary;
Praise Him in His mighty expanse.
Praise Him for His mighty deeds; praise Him according to His excellent greatness.
Let everything that has breath, praise the Lord!"

Psalm 150:1,2,6

Through praise, we can draw closer to God. Scripture says in Psalm 100:4a, "Enter His gates with thanksgiving and His courts with praise." When we praise, we can enter God's presence. Imagine your relationship with a beloved friend or relative. How does time together strengthen your bond? This time in the presence of God helps us know Him more. We feel His heart and start to hear His voice more clearly—all from being around Him. The term "praise reports" refers to things we notice God did, for which we celebrate. They are spiritual activities that we tell others, testifying that God showed up. These testimonies bring faith to the hearers and create within us an expectation that He will do it again.

When we praise God, it keeps us from spiraling into upset and overwhelming negative emotions. The enemy wants to whisper worse case scenarios every chance he has, asking relentless "what ifs." Praise keeps us from that spiral and prevents discouragement.

> "It is good to give thanks to the Lord and to sing praises to Your name, O Most High; to declare Your lovingkindness in the morning, and Your faithfulness by night."
>
> Psalm 92:1-2

Worship, praise, and thanksgiving all go hand in hand. They are ways of expression that release our love and devotion to God, testifying of His goodness. Thanksgiving is a lifestyle that has multiple scriptures supporting it. The beauty of gratitude is once you start thanking God for His goodness in your life, you'll see it everywhere.

When I go to bed, I thank God for things that took place throughout the day. My list has no parameters on it. It includes anything that is good. I expect to see my day go well, because I invite

Jesus into everything I do. Even if the unexpected arises, I still trust in Him.

My husband and I drove our two cars to the shop. I dropped off one and rode with him in the other. He said, "Do you hear that rumble?" I said, "Yes, that doesn't sound good." He pulled into the bank parking lot, and I got out to look around and saw we had a flat tire. Our auto mechanic, who also has a tire shop, was right across the street. We were able to drive our car there at 9:00 p.m. and leave it. We mentioned it to guys working there after hours. Then, we walked home, roughly a mile. It was incredible how everything worked out. The day before this happened, I was thirty miles away from home. Thank you, Lord, it didn't happen then!

I also thank the Lord for shopping bargains and sales. I find crazy deals! Recently, I decided I wanted a zipper front robe. The day came when I went shopping to look for it. A store I like had one red winter robe, my size, at seventy-five percent off! Yes, I bought it, thank you Lord.

Sharing these stories are a reminder God wants to interact with our everyday life and not be compartmentalized into what we deem as spiritual. It is easy to give God thanks for people being saved, healed, and delivered. It is easy to give God thanks after witnessing His power touching another's life. As a short-term missionary, I have seen His power at work in other countries. From limbs growing out to blind eyes seeing, deaf ears hearing, back pain disappearing, wheelchairs being left behind, and more. While in India preaching at a village church, my friend and I were invited into a concrete building while a woman lay there on an elevated surface, ready to die. Bugs and flies were swarming around her. My friend began to command a spirit of death to leave and spoke life into her. We later learned this woman completely recovered! Praise God!

In addition to blessings and miracles, we can give God thanks for situations that have His favor on them. The list is endless of things for which we can thank God. The more you give thanks, the more you see His involvement. From the smallest of details like finding lost keys, to the largest like raising the dead. The closer we are to Him, the more we are aware of His goodness flowing through all areas of our life. The more we are thankful, the more our eyes are opened to His goodness.

My husband is a family physician who served in the Army for eleven years. After his residency, we were called to serve in Baumholder, Germany. We had three young children at the time. After some research, we learned that this duty station had eight months of winter and service members said it was very isolated. Our household furniture was shipped, and sometime later we learned our orders had been changed to Vicenza, Italy. It was certainly a time to celebrate and thank God! Our tour in Italy was fabulous.

> "It is good to give thanks to the Lord and to sing praises to Your name, O Most High; to declare Your lovingkindness in the morning, and Your faithfulness by night."
>
> Psalm 92:1-2

It is one thing to give God thanks when there is an overt reason. It is quite another to give thanks when the chips are down, disappointment sets in, or prayers are not answered. The enemy comes and whispers that God does not care—that you are not loved and your troubles don't concern Him. There are times when we must walk by faith, and know that even when life is upside down, God is with us and will help us if we ask.

I used to minister in assisted living homes for ten years. Each year near thanksgiving, the Lord would have me speak on being thankful. I recall the first time He said this, I responded, "What do these people have to be thankful for?" He replied, "If anyone is breathing, they have something to be thankful for." Then the Lord gave me a list of things for which to be grateful while living in a nursing home: people to care for you, friends, food, a warm bed, activities, and more.

Living with an attitude of gratitude produces joy. Being thankful when things don't go our way keeps our eyes on Jesus and not our circumstances. We can always be thankful for His love, faithfulness, abiding presence, wisdom, grace, protection, peace, and so much more.

> "Rejoice always; pray without ceasing; in everything give thanks, for this is God's will for you in Christ Jesus."
>
> 1 Thessalonians 5:16-18

Praise, worship, and thanksgiving are all ways to come into the presence of God. Setting our mind and heart upon Him, these expressions show adoration and love. Just as there are food staples we keep in our kitchen these are relationship necessities. The more we honor the Lord, the more our troubles grow dim. This is a sure-fire way to grow closer to Him. Keeping praise, worship, and thanksgiving a priority in your life will help you stay steadfast in your relationship with God.

Chapter Nuggets

- "Worship involves intimacy and submission."
- We worship God for who He is.
- Praise celebrates God for what He has done.
- Praise produces joy, which is a strength.
- Thanksgiving is an expression testifying of God's goodness.
- A developed habit of thanksgiving will result in seeing God's goodness all over our lives.
- Keeping praise, worship, and thanksgiving a priority in your life will help you stay close to God.

CHAPTER 5

Compartmentalization

One fine day, I had a revelation about life and ministry. I was with my father, and we were visiting my mother in a dementia care unit. At some point I recall thinking, "This feels like ministry." I used to minister in rest homes, so maybe that started the revelation. At that moment, the Lord began to reveal how I compartmentalize life and ministry.

Compartmentalizing describes the act of dividing tasks into categories for accomplishing what we need to do. Just like people compartmentalize the priorities and pleasures of life, sometimes we put God in a compartment. Sundays we go to church, and we present our Sunday best. After we come home from church we jump back into life as usual, and God is put aside for the week. There may be a Wednesday night service, youth group, or prayer meeting we attend. Considering the hours in a week—one hundred sixty-eight—how many of those hours do we surrender to Jesus? The following verse suggests we live attached.

> "I am the vine, you are the branches; he who abides in Me and I in him, he bears much fruit, for apart from Me, you can do nothing."
>
> John 15:5

As a minister, I used to compartmentalize God. When I was serving; preaching, teaching Sunday school, doing missions work, leading Bible study, outreaching, or holding prayer meetings, I considered my ministry valuable to God and counted as important. Tending to my family, doing chores, shopping, and going on vacations were categorized differently. I was either serving God or doing life. Serving God had merit and doing life did not. In fact, Jesus was not interested in my life nearly as much as He was interested in how I could serve Him. This was my erroneous belief.

In our current day, this belief system would limit God working through individuals in their

Compartmentalization

workplace, school environment, family, media, or anywhere else. If we chose only to engage the Lord while doing "ministry," and not allow Him access to all areas, we are limiting His grace, His divine assistance.

My daughter is an avid cross-training athlete and has participated in multiple competitions. Caitlin is also credentialed to be a personal trainer. During her fitness journey, she has learned many skills and lifts that appear in cross-training workouts. There was a particular movement, however, that she could not get. It's called a "bar muscle-up." Although coaches told her she had the strength to do the movement, something about the execution just didn't click.

After months of being unable to do bar muscle-ups, Caitlin got serious. She set a goal to perform her first muscle-up by the end of January and started focused practice. She says, "On the last day of January, I walked into the gym. God had showed me a new tip that I wanted to try. On my first attempt that day, I floated to the top of the bar. It was almost as though I didn't know what was happening. At the top of the bar, I rejoiced! It was nothing short of a miracle. The movement felt completely different than what I had been trying to do. God truly taught my body how to do it. It was God's divine involvement through His amazing love for me. He is the ultimate coach!"

When our oldest daughter was getting married, we went shopping for my dress. Before we began, I asked for God's help and guidance. By noon I was hungry. We hustled through the dress department just grabbing dresses that might work. I tried on four. The one I liked was one hundred sixty dollars. I said to my daughter, "Is this on sale?" I did not want to pay that cost. We looked around and did not see a sale sign. Then I heard the Lord say to wait in a particular checkout line, which I did. "Is this on sale?" I asked the cashier. She replied, "Today we are playing roulette. You can choose an option of twenty percent off, or you can play roulette, where the cash register picks the percentage off."

I chose roulette. Guess what? I received one hundred percent off! I got a brand new one-hundred-sixty-dollar dress for free! I have never seen this department store play this game again. I was so thankful to God.

Compartmentalization

My dear friends went on a serious weight-loss journey. This husband and wife sought the Lord for their weight-loss lifestyle change. Between their research and God's direction, they found a program that provides a menu based on bloodwork. It has been two years, and they remain successful in their endeavors. They realize it is a lifestyle change, and they want to continue living healthy and strong, serving the Lord. God is giving them grace to continue making wise eating decisions.

In marriage, I found out early that God was not interested in my prayers for changing my husband. The longer my husband and I argued about who was right and who was wrong, the more the enemy divided us. We both learned from God and through practice, to forgive quickly and take time to listen and hear the intentions of one another. Conflict is unavoidable in marriage. But through forgiveness, it can be resolved.

The Lord has shown me that I used to attach value to ministry endeavors and not to family, nor anything else in life. I thought that God was more pleased when I taught a Bible study than when I played with my kids or read them bedtime stories.

The only thing that had value in life was ministry related. This theory started to break down when I began taking care of my elderly parents.

"Whether then you eat or drink, or whatever you do, do all to the glory of God."

1 Corinthians 10:31

Looking at life through the lens of the kingdom, you will find that the Lord is not using a value system. He is interested in all our activities as well as our personal endeavors. Our personal transformation is as important as ministry accomplishments. Our internal development is highly important because that affects all the externals. He has no interest in being compartmentalized; He wants our whole being.

I realize exceptionally gifted people can execute plans, relying on their own ability instead of inviting the Lord to participate; however, if we invite His help into those areas of our expertise, we will see His fruitful results. What God can produce surpasses what we can do on our own.

Money can easily take God's place in our hearts. This is why it is vitally important to have God's leading in how we use our resources. He

Compartmentalization

asks us to give so money does not control us. It is easy to get into serious debt, easy to spend frivolously, to buy things impulsively, to not have any discipline over it. God's word says, "Give and it shall be given to you, pressed down, shaken together and running over," Luke 6:38. Giving unto the Lord keeps money from having a hold on us, plus providing for the kingdom to advance.

My husband prays over our finances and while he does research, the Lord gives him the necessary wisdom to make good decisions. The word tells us in James 1:5, "But if any of you lacks wisdom, let him ask of God, who gives to all generously and without reproach, and it will be given to him." Finances are a great area to have surrendered to the Lord. We have been financially blessed as we have been faithful in our giving.

"Now this I say, he who sows sparingly will also reap sparingly, and he who sows bountifully will also reap bountifully. Each one must do just as he purposed in his heart, not grudgingly or under compulsion, for God loves a cheerful giver."

2 Corinthians 9:6-7

I share these stories because God's desire is partnership in every compartment of life, not just what we call, "ministry." The Holy Spirit is an abiding presence—with us in every activity. It is on us to invite His participation as we go through our day.

When I realized the Lord valued all my life's activities and not just ministry assignments, I found myself in greater levels of joy. If you think He only values ministry, you will miss the fullness of your relationship. In this family partnership, we are already accepted and significant, and do not need to earn our worth.

I believe God also likes to watch His kids play and have fun, just as I enjoy playing with my grandkids on vacation. As I have removed compartments and now include Jesus into our vacations, the enjoyment has increased. Our souls need play and I feel God's pleasure on this. We can invite the Lord's presence into every activity.

Sometimes, I wonder how anyone navigates life without the brilliance of God. We truly need Him in all areas, not just a church compartment. Our Maker and Creator wants to infuse us with His new life, bringing us peace during chaos, joy amidst troubles, and love that fulfills our hearts.

Compartmentalization

He is calling His people to come closer so He can refresh and renew. Closer to Him ultimately means a greater dependence, a greater surrender, and greater passion for Christ—even in everyday tasks.

Chapter Nuggets

- People compartmentalize God.
- Ministry is not more important to God than other areas of life.
- Give Jesus access to all areas of life.
- All of life has value.
- Our worth is not based on performance, but as a son or daughter.
- If you think God only values ministry, you will miss the fullness of your relationship.
- Our Maker wants to infuse all our life with His love, peace, and joy.

CHAPTER 6

Community

I was a hospital chaplain for two years. While serving, I would visit patients and ask if they wanted prayer. I lost count of the number of people who said they loved Jesus but did not belong to any church. After further discussion the issue of being hurt by a church member always came up. I then encouraged people to forgive and visit other church families.

I understand that hurt, offense, or mistreatment can happen and is very real. It is a touchy subject, and at the time it occurs, the easiest way out is to leave the church. Changing churches due to offense, however, carries the offense to the next church. God will help you forgive and give you wisdom and timing for talking to those who hurt you. Sometimes, a mediator is necessary. If God calls you to move to another church—and He may—it is best to leave after repairing the hurt.

Even with the possibility of hurt or offense, I encourage everyone to find a church family. There is a time for personal study, and there is a time for corporate gatherings. I would be amiss to suggest that we can stay near to God and continue to draw closer without some form of community. A gathering of believers is meant to represent a family of God that helps us with our identity in Christ, discipleship, and calling.

Church is a place to be taught the word of God—a place to serve, practice your gifts, and understand your purpose in Christ. Fellow church members can cheer us on, pray with us, and teach us. You don't need to be perfect, none of us are, to participate in this wonderful community. Ann Landers, an advice columnist, once said, "Church is not a museum of saints, but a hospital for sinners."

> "...and let us consider how to stimulate one another to love and good deeds, not forsaking our own assembling together, as is the habit of

some, but encouraging one another; and all the more as you see the day drawing near."

Hebrews 10:24-25

Bill Johnson says about Bethel Church: "This is a place of training for deployment." The church disciples' believers. After salvation, which is just the beginning of our journey with Christ, there is the teaching and equipping to become Christlike aligning ourselves with the kingdom of Heaven in the great commandment and the great commission.

When it comes to selecting a church, there are multiple denominations. The big difference is non-denominational versus denominational. My family has been to both. I grew up in a Lutheran church and met my husband there. After marriage, we traveled with the military. We experienced multiple denominations: Lutheran, Methodist, Baptist, Army Chapel, Evangelical Free, and even a Seventh-Day Adventist church.

While we began with the denominational church, the Lord eventually directed us to a non-denominational church, and this has been our fit. The primary difference between the two is how they view the Holy Spirit. Many non-denominational churches believe in the gifts of the Holy Spirt and welcome His spontaneous participation in service. The preaching of the word itself is very important; however, the power of the Holy Spirit is also very much needed in our spiritual growth. I encourage you to pray and seek the Lord for which church family is right for you.

Size is a consideration when church shopping. There are house churches cropping up for those who enjoy an intimate group and living life together. The mega church is at the other end of the spectrum, where thousands gather to hear the word of the Lord. I have experienced small and large churches. It is easy to know everyone in the small church, and to be involved. The large church has more ministries in operation, and small groups as a way for people to get to know one another. The Holy Spirit is attracted to both, so you may pray and decide which to attend.

Another help in determining your church home is meeting with the Pastor. Today we have online services to watch, so that's informative. Getting together with the Pastor and hearing His vison for the church, community involvement, and even about his calling to Pastor is all good information. The passions in your heart should align with the vision of the church and get you excited. The church we go to is heavily involved with supporting missionaries and that excites me, because I travel for the Lord. Our church makes room for the Holy Spirit to save, heal and deliver. We also have a prayer room, and prayer is a priority.

When Covid hit our nation and churches went into lockdown, people became familiar with watching services online. The plus side to this is churches who previously lacked this technology now have online services available. We can watch sermons all over the world. While this may be convenient for some, it does not have the same impact. When we attend church in person, we experience a stronger sense of God's presence, better focus, and connection with others—like family celebrating together. Imagine watching a sporting event versus being there in person: it is not nearly the same experience.

Foundational to a healthy church is the prayer life of that church. In Isaiah 56:7b, God says, "For My house will be called a house of prayer for all peoples." Considering the different personalities, ethnicities, and ages of people coming together to worship and engage with the Lord, there is bound to be friction. Prayer helps keep the church on track with God's purposes and provides a place for God to speak prophetically to the church.

Church is a place to discover and grow in your gifts. There are multiple ways to serve, be involved, and learn how to partner with the Lord. Try different ministries and see what develops. My first act of service in the church at twenty years old was helping in the nursery. Then I became an usher. I kept trying things and stepping up where there was a need and eventually found myself in prayer, preaching, and teaching roles. Now, I am on the prophetic team, ministry team, mission's council, and lead teams on missionary trips.

How does the church draw us closer to God? We engage in worship, hear the word, receive prayer, encourage friends, see evidence of salvations, healings, and miracles—all which draw us closer to God's heart. Involvement increases our desire for the Lord. My husband and I are on the ministry and prophetic teams, and we see many people touched by the power of the

Holy Spirit. This fuels our passion to know Him more.

The phrase, "I am not being fed," is a common reason for people to leave the church. While this may be true, our participation is for the benefit of our church family. Coming only for the purpose of receiving is too fattening. Our volunteering in our church gives way to learning, growing, and blessing.

I highly recommend having a church family. It is incredibly helpful to have friends and mentors to cheer us on in our walk with Jesus. Just as important is our opportunity to cheer others on. I have been in church all my life, growing in my understanding of the word, identity, and giftings. A community of believers, worshipping together, hearing the uncompromised word, and receiving prayer is beneficial to our discipleship development.

Chapter Nuggets

- Church community helps us grow in discipleship, identity, and calling.
- You can always interview the Pastor before committing to a church family.
- Church is a place to be taught the word of God-a place to serve, practice your gifts and serve, practice your gifts, and understand your purpose I Christ.
- Non-Denominational church makes room for the Holy Spirit.
- Leaving a church offended carries that offense to the next church.
- Online services do not have the same presence as being there.
- Prayer is foundational to a healthy church.

CHAPTER 7

Fasting

Recently, I went on a three-day fast for a street ministry outreach trip. I fasted for the Lord to accomplish His mission through us. Throughout the trip, we felt the presence of the Lord. We spoke with one hundred twenty-five people, all of them welcoming. We prayed for healing, gave encouraging words, handed out books including a Bible, gave soup to a homeless ministry, blessed a Pastor with funds, ministered in a nursing home, and prayed at the highest peak in Pennsylvania. We saw the Holy Spirit fill people with joy and hope. He led us every step of the way. We even missed a rainstorm. It was a glorious trip!

Fasting is a powerful tool to help keep us aligned with the Kingdom of God. My personal experience with fasting is ongoing. I expect to fast periodically until the end of my lifetime. There are many good reasons to fast, and we have biblical accounts of why fasting achieves powerful results. Whether you've fasted before, are currently practicing, or are hearing about it for the first time, I highly recommend it.

In the book of Esther, a three-day fast saves the Jewish nation. Esther was promoted to queen in the place of Queen Vashti, after the latter had turned down the request of King Ahasuerus to appear at the end of a week-long celebration. Queen Vashti was banished from the presence of the king after her refusal. Esther, a Jew, raised by her uncle, Mordecai, eventually becomes chosen to be queen.

There was an evil plot by one of the king's officials, Haman. He set out to destroy the Jews. Haman coerced the king in signing an edict to annihilate the Jewish people. Mordecai found out and relayed the message to Esther. He asked her to petition the king on behalf of their people—to save their lives from slaughter. This is a significant request, because the custom was as follows: if the queen was not summoned by the

Fasting

king, she would go to him in fear for her life. If the king did not hold out the golden scepter when the queen spontaneously came to speak, she was sentenced to death.

When Esther expresses concern about appearing before the king uninvited, Mordecai responds: "For if you remain silent at this time, relief and deliverance will arise for the Jews from another place and you and your father's house will perish. And who knows whether you have not attained royalty for such a time as this?" (Esther 4:14)

Esther's response was to call a fast: no eating or drinking for three days. The fast was for all the Jews in Suza. Esther declares, "If I perish, I perish." After the fast, Esther goes to the king. She has favor and he extends the golden scepter. Esther reveals Haman's plot to destroy the Jews.

Here in this story, a three-day fast saved a nation. A corporate fast such as this, where people's lives are at stake, is serious business. God moved on behalf of His people, honoring the fast, and the wickedness of Haman was exposed. In the end, Haman lost his life. The enemy was defeated, the honorable Mordecai was promoted, and Esther kept her favor with the king.

Fasting helps us focus and makes it easier to hear from God. I have found that it helps remove clutter and busyness from my mind. Prayer and Bible study should accompany it. If the activity of your day of fasting is not slowed down—if your schedule is no different than any other day—that may be more of a hunger strike. Fast when you can adjust your activity level and when you have extra time to spend with the Lord. It is not a day to go to the gym, run a few miles, or build a house. Slow down and be prepared to hear from Heaven.

"Then Jesus was led up by the Spirit into the wilderness to be tempted by the devil. And after He had fasted forty days and forty nights, He then became hungry," (Matthew 4:1-2). Jesus' forty-day fast had a purpose in defeating the devil's temptations against His identity. The devil kept repeating, "If you are the Son of God," Prior to this wilderness experience, God affirmed Jesus as His beloved Son at His baptism. Jesus' ministry began after this victorious wilderness testing, and the fasting strengthened Him. If Jesus fasted and overcame temptation, we can do likewise.

Fasting

A famous prophet went to work at a hospital for mentally handicapped children, hundreds of them, who were discarded by their parents. He met a sixteen-year-old boy who had multiple problems: down's syndrome, moderate retardation, physical deformities, and self-mutilation. He would beat himself in the face. The hospital tried shock treatment to no avail.

Under the Lord's direction, the prophet fasted for fourteen days. After which, he was in his office and called the boy in. When he prayed, the boy was instantly delivered and in his right mind. This fast was called forth by God, and the prophet obeyed. The Lord told him to fast, and in that fast, God equipped him to deliver the boy.

Fasting is a powerful tool for deliverance. Breakthrough and freedom can come by fasting. Setting our sights on the word of God and believing His word over our trouble, while we fast, brings a laser-like focus for breaking strongholds.

"When they came to the crowd, a man came up to Jesus, falling on his knees before him and saying, 'Lord, have mercy on my son, for he is a lunatic and very ill; for he often falls into the fire and often into the water. I brought him to your disciples, and they could not cure him.'"

Matthew 17:14-16

The disciples and Jesus have a conversation about the failure of the disciples to set the boy free. Jesus says it is because of the "littleness" of their faith, then he also mentions, "But this kind does not go out except by prayer and fasting," (Matthew 17:21). Fasting engages the power of God to a higher degree than prayer alone.

Corporate fasts are taking place all over our nation. Churches, prayer groups, and ministries are fasting for our country to repent and turn back to God. I believe a mighty move of God has begun, and we will see revival sweep through the highways and byways.

Fasting can bring us godly wisdom and a new heavenly perspective. It clears away the clutter in our mind and helps us hear how to receive from God. Align your heart before your fast, and check if it is a fast for His purposes. We won't always see immediate results—like fasting for our country's salvation-but we can trust our fast is making a difference.

Fasting

There are many ways to fast: food, sweets, meat, news, phone, or whatever you decide. I prefer a shorter fast and no food. You can fast as Daniel did and only eat vegetables and fruit. Or you can give up food, drinking your calories instead. You can fast television or social media. Whatever you choose, enter your fast with specifics, and take time to journal what you hear from the Lord. This draws you closer to Him.

If you feel yourself losing your love for the Lord, fast and ask for renewed love and compassion. You can also fast for renewed strength. God will move on those things quickly. . I fast for my mission's trips, to clearly hear the word He has for the nation I am traveling to. Also, for an outpouring of the Holy Spirit.

Anything you want to add emphasis on in the kingdom, you can fast about. You can fast to draw closer to God. You can fast about an assignment, healing, deliverance, finances, any number of things. I fast one day a week, Mondays, when I am home. Our country is always on my fast list. Occasionally, I will extend it to three days but if it goes longer than that, I fast certain food groups instead of abstaining from all.

I experience a closeness to the Lord when I fast and pray. It reminds me of a football huddle, only just between God and I. We come together, our eyes are upon one another, and it is time to listen to the play. When you hear from the Master Himself, it produces an assurance in your heart that God has spoken and made clear how to proceed. Any time there are major decisions to make—a geographical move, a new job, a ministry assignment—fasting is a great way to get clarity.

Fasting brings us into a humble posture, relying on God's breakthrough strength as we submit to Him. As the angel said to Mary, "For nothing will be impossible with God," (Luke 1:37). Faith increases as we pay attention to the word. A resolve is birthed. Mary responded, "...may it be done to me according to Your word," (Luke 1:38b). If the Lord is leading you into a fast, go for it. If He is not, you may still initiate one. Your breakthrough may be one fast away!

Fasting

Chapter Nuggets

- Fasting is a powerful tool to help keep us aligned with the Kingdom of God.
- While fasting, allow room in your schedule to spend extra time to listen, pray, and read His word.
- Jesus' fast in the wilderness helped defeat the enemy, preparing Him for ministry.
- Fasting brings focus, removing distractions.
- Fasting brings clarity.
- Fasting provides increased strength for casting out demons.
- Fasting is great for major decisions needing clarity from the Lord.

CLOSER

CHAPTER 8

Navigate Disappointment

My husband was an officer and a doctor in the U.S. Army. He had a very demanding assignment overseas and his primary purpose, beyond patient care, was making his commanding officer look good and making his commanding officer's life easier. He had accomplished this in his first two years of the assignment. When his commanding officer was due to transfer, he told my husband he could not give him recognition before he left, but he promised he would relay the information to his successor: that my husband deserved a certain level of recognition, and he would have bestowed it if he remained in the position.

When it came time for us to transfer, my husband received the minimum recognition any officer could get in his circumstance. The new commanding officer felt he could not justify the higher level of recognition and, likely, wanted to reserve this recognition for officers who served *him* better, not someone else.

It was a massive disappointment for my husband after working long hours for three years—being promised something special and not receiving it. He was very "down" when at an event recognizing transferring officers, he received his minimal military recognition. Then, to his surprise, he was showered with love by his colleagues and coworkers who presented him with a beautiful memory photograph with personal remembrances. He also received an outpouring of love from his patients, including one family who gave him a porcelain serving tray.

My husband realized his identity was not what the Army said about him, but what God says about him. We can all hear God, but often we hear better when God uses other people to reinforce His love for us. We are in transition now, but when we have a house again these two keepsakes will resume a place of honor as "standing stones" in my husband's and my life—reminders of the good things God has done.

Disappointment is one of the greatest challenges of the Christian faith, causing some to turn away from the very One who can redeem their situation. People who have believed God and have not seen their desired results lose their trust. Life with Jesus is not a guarantee against disappointment. Rather, it is a walk of faith and belief that even though circumstances appear defeating, we can hold fast to God and expect Him to redeem us.

The biblical story of Joseph is a prime example of overcoming disappointment. He had dreams about ruling over his family and told his brothers. Afterward, his brothers plotted against him. They dumped him into a well, then rescued him to sell to traders. Joseph was hauled off to Egypt. The brothers—to conceal their wrongdoing—dipped Joseph's tunic in goat blood and took it to their father, Jacob, who mourned for his son for many days. Meanwhile, Joseph was taken down to Egypt and Potiphar, an Egyptian officer, bought him.

"The Lord was with Joseph, so he became a successful man. And he was in the house of his master, the Egyptian. Now his master saw that the Lord was with him and how the Lord caused all that he did to prosper. So, Joseph found favor in his sight and became his personal servant; and he made him overseer over his house, and all that he owned he put in his charge. So, he left everything he owned in Jospeh's charge, and with him there, he did not concern himself with anything except the food which he ate. Now, Jospeh was handsome in form and appearance."

Genesis 39:2-4, 6

Potiphar's wife goes after Joseph, wanting him to lie with her. He runs away but she is left holding his cloak. She then accuses Joseph of pursuing a physical relationship with her, and Potiphar puts him in jail.

Here is where everything appears to fall apart for Joseph. He went from the palace to jail. He had favor, trust, and responsibility, but false accusations lost Joseph his favorable position.

This is one picture of disappointment. Living in the Lord's favor and losing it because of a lie. Where is the justification? Where is the vindication? Where is God? This is where you and I have a choice: we can either turn to our flesh, crying out, "Injustice!" or we can turn the situation over to God, trusting Him to work through it with us. If we choose to respond God's way, we forgive our offenders and allow God to heal our hearts.

There is an erroneous belief that God uses sickness and disease to teach us, but Jesus healed everyone who came to Him. Many Christians still believe everything that happens in life is because "God allows it." This thought can lead to blaming God for hardships. Disappointments can become offenses toward God, building walls around our heart that hinders our freedom and relationship with Him.

On this side of Heaven, we will not have all the answers. There are several reasons why things don't work out the way we plan. We could be praying out of God's will. The disciples wanted to call down fire, and Jesus said, "You do not know what kind of spirit you are of: for the Son of Man did not come to destroy men's lives, but to save them," (Luke 9:55-56).

We could be out of God's timing. We are an impatient, instantaneous society. No one wants to wait; no one wants to go through the process of preparation. We call it, "waiting on God." God does not waste time. During our periods of waiting, He builds our character. Joseph had time to process his mistreatment while in prison, and he did so God's way.

Christian leaders all experience disappointment in ministry at some point. Years ago, I began holding meetings in a hotel on Sunday mornings for the hotel guests. An incomplete idea I realize now, but I went for it. After six months, my husband said, "This is not working." He pointed out that people who are traveling for the weekend are usually not looking for a Sunday morning service in their hotel. I was disappointed to find out my idea, which I believed to be God's was not bearing fruit. I did surmise, I should have prayed into this more. Disappointments can be the result of improper preparation.

Besides ministry, there are disappointments interwoven throughout every area of life. In all these things, let us remind ourselves that "...neither death, nor life, nor angels, nor principalities, nor things present, nor things to come, nor powers, nor height, nor depth, nor any other created thing, will be able to separate us from the love of God, which is in Christ Jesus our Lord," (Romans 8:38b-39). You and I are the only ones that can separate us from the love of God; one way we can do that is through our response to disappointment or losing hope.

Within our personal countries, we can be disappointed in government, educational systems, media, churches, journalists, health systems, border control, and the list goes on. We have a choice to make regarding disappointment. Option one, is we can crawl in a hole and allow it to draw us away from the Lord, becoming offended and getting fixated on the 'Why did this happen to me?" Option two, we can hunker down with the Lord, repent, remove offense through forgiveness, and allow Him to heal our hearts, and renew our vision.

Joseph, in his hardship, proceeded to keep a godly frame of mind. "But the Lord was with Joseph and extended kindness to him and gave him favor in the sight of the chief jailor. The chief jailor committed to Joseph's charge all the prisoners who were in the jail; so that whatever was done there, he was responsible for it. The chief jailor did not supervise anything under Joseph's charge because the Lord was with him; and whatever he did, the Lord made to prosper," (Genesis 39:21-23).

It is important to note that the Lord was with Joseph, even during his jail time. The Lord does not leave us when we are in difficulty. Instead of the Lord immediately delivering Joseph out of prison, the Lord brought Jospeh to an elevated place *while* in prison. Our response to the Lord should not be blaming and complaining—showing a lack of trust—but one of drawing closer to Him. May we listen to his voice on how to posture ourselves in a godly way. This is an uplifting response to disappointment. Will we hang on to the Lord even while not understanding?

The Bible tells us in Romans 12:2: "And do not be conformed to this world but be transformed by the renewing of your mind." The renewed mind will recognize the voice of the enemy and cast it off. Agreeing with destructive thinking empowers those thoughts. God is gracious as we grapple with disappointment and work through it. Surrendering the entire situation to the Lord—along with the disappointment—will allow His grace to help us through.

I heard a story about a prophet who in his younger years, during ministry school, heard of his mother becoming mentally ill. He quit school to go home and help. His dad was a pastor who left the church because of her illness and began a grueling job with long work hours. Eventually, the mental illness took her life. The devil will come with accusations to turn us away from the very One who can heal and redeem us. The prophet and another brother hung on to the Lord. The other two brothers left the Lord and one of them ended up in jail.

In the next stage of Joseph's story, both Pharaoh's cupbearer and baker were put in prison. They were looking sad one day, so Joseph asked them what was wrong. They each had a dream but no one to interpret it. Joseph accurately interpreted their dreams, with a request that they remember him. He still carried hope for his release. We always have hope, for Jesus is our hope. Although it may take a hit at times, hope can always be renewed.

Eventually, the chief cupbearer had an opportunity to mention Joseph to Pharoah. "Yet the chief cupbearer did not remember Joseph but forgot him," (Genesis 40:23). Another dash to Joseph's hopes. Another disappointment. Yet, God was still with him. Finally, Joseph's prison term was coming to an end. Pharoah had a dream, and no one could interpret it. At this point, the chief cupbearer remembered Joseph. He is brought before Pharoah to interpret the dream, and he is accurate.

"So, Pharoah said to Joseph, 'Since God has informed you of all this, there is no one so discerning and wise as you are. You shall be over my house, and according to your command all my people shall do homage; only in the throne I will be greater than you.' Pharoah said to Joseph, 'See I have set you over all the land of Egypt.'"
Genesis 41:39-41

The redemption of Joseph's disappointments is amazing. The goodness of God restored all the heartache and loss. Joseph's family eventually came to reunite with him in Egypt, and they moved there. The reason this story has a happy ending is because Joseph remained faithful to God, even in prison. He was able to forgive his brothers when they showed up. Did God plan all those events? No. God did not plan for Joseph to be sold and unfairly placed in prison. Likewise, the dashed hopes and disappointments we face are not planned by God either. But only He can heal our wounds, our hearts, our minds, and restore hope. God can restore any circumstance as we surrender it to Him and invite Him into our situation. He is our Redeemer.

Living close to God will keep us faithful and hopeful during times of disappointments. He will be the one we cling to, not alienate. He will be the one we trust to bring restoration and healing, rather than be angry and walk away. It is said that we grow more in the valleys than on the mountaintops. Every disappointment and setback can be a setup into the greater plans the Lord has, just like the story of Joseph.

Chapter Nuggets

- If we respond God's way, we forgive our offenders and allow God to heal our hearts.
- There is an erroneous belief that God uses sickness to teach us.
- Nothing separates us from God's love, except us.
- Joseph's favor resulted from faithfulness.
- Choose to forgive and let God heal your heart.
- Living close to God will keep us faithful and hopeful in times of disappointment.
- God can use setbacks as setups into His greater plans.

CHAPTER 9

Receive and Release Love

"...God is love..." 1 John 4:16

This past year I had the honor of speaking at a pastors and leaders conference in Africa. My message was *"Five Reasons to Draw Closer to God."* The night before I was to speak, I had an encounter with the Holy Spirit. During the early morning hours, I was awake and began thinking about my message. Soon I found myself weeping for those to whom I would speak. My heart was flooded with God's love for His people. This went on for about two hours. After that I didn't sleep.

Morning came, and I was still a bit weepy, so my leader gave me the first session. While I was sharing, I felt the love of God for the congregation. I believe they felt it also. The altar had a great response, and I cried with many people that day. The team leader said, "It was a breakthrough meeting." God's love saturated participants' hearts and they received the message of drawing closer to Him. I don't think we fully understand the depth of God's love and how it breaks through darkness to reach into the deepest recesses of our being.

Love is the core of the Christian faith. There is no other religion in which love is the essence of the god. Scripture tells us that love is the reason Jesus came. "For God so loved the world, that He gave His only begotten Son, that whoever believes in Him shall not perish, but have eternal life," (John 3:16). Jesus came to restore mankind's sinful condition and reconcile us to Father God.

Unfortunately, the world has watered down the word "love" into a feeling, attributing it to many areas. We love food, houses, movies, vacations, jobs, clothes, cars, money, furniture, or any number of materialistic items. While God is not opposed to us having nice things; He is opposed to things having a stronger place in our hearts than He does. "But seek first His kingdom, and His righteousness, and all these things shall be added unto you," (Matthew 6:33). As we seek first His kingdom and right standing with Him, He will take care of the things we need.

Our connection to God is our life source, the fulfilment of our heart, the very thing for which people are searching. As we grow closer to God, our understanding of His love for us increases. The world needs us to share this revelation. When there is an absence of love, that void can attach to unhealthy counterfeits. When there is an absence of love in the family, children will look elsewhere to fill that void.

Statistics show that fatherlessness affects children to the degree that they become criminals, ending up in jail. The importance of a loving, healthy relationship in the family speaks volumes for a healthy life. Fathers are their kids' first understanding of the love of Father God. The demonstration of love in the home will have a positive effect, while a demonstration of abuse will have a painful one.

> "...and behold a voice out of the heavens said, 'This is my beloved Son, in whom I am well pleased.'"
>
> Matthew 3:17

Prior to Jesus beginning his earthly ministry, He was baptized by John the Baptist. Take note that God spoke His love over Jesus, as a "beloved Son," when He had not yet done any ministry. This is where many of us miss it. We believe that we must work to earn God's love, striving to prove that we are worthy of His affections. Some of us, on the other hand, believe that no matter how hard we try, we miss the mark—that we are not worthy of receiving His love, or that our "brownie points" never add up to being enough.

On our own merit, no one is good enough to receive eternal life. That is exactly why Jesus died for us. He became the perfect sacrifice to restore us back to the Father, taking the penalty of sin upon Himself. Jesus did for us what we could not do ourselves. When I think about what my salvation cost Jesus, I want my life to count for His suffering.

This was where I got into trouble. My love language is service. I would evaluate my service unto the Lord and found myself lacking in my own eyes as to the fruit I was bearing. I kept hearing this voice say I was not doing enough to pay Jesus back for His sacrifice. I found myself striving, trying to do more and more to satisfy the nagging feeling of, "Jesus is not receiving the rewards of His suffering."

This is all connected to an orphan spirit. Once I began learning about the orphan spirit versus sonship, I realized I was an orphan: one who did not fully receive my acceptance into God's family without working for it. The freedom that came from accepting my identity as a much beloved daughter transformed my life and walk with God. It brought an incredible freedom and a new understanding of my personal relationship.

When we look at our kids, we are happy to see them play and enjoy themselves. In fact, we are happy watching them sleep. If the only time our kids communicated with us was to ask for chores, something would be wrong. While our service to the Lord is important, He is more interested in who we are becoming.

"For you have not received a spirit of slavery leading to fear again, but you have received a spirit of adoption as sons by which we cry out, 'Abba Father!'"

Romans 8:15

Our identity in Christ is one of sonship. Through Him, we become an adopted son or daughter in the Father's family. We live by faith and His empowering grace, instead of performance, and work. We are God's children, and we belong. We are already accepted the day we receive Jesus as our Savior. This partnership is amazing. As a son or daughter of God, our life is lived with unconditional love, acceptance, value and worth. We must prove nothing. We are forgiven and redeemed by the blood of Christ.

No matter our past, once we come into the family of God, we have significance. Our circumstances do not define us, nor our wealth, poverty, or reputation. We are freely forgiven for all sin, and the slate is wiped clean. What a great way to begin our new life in Christ! Then, God's love begins to transform our hearts. No longer do we live like the world, but we align ourselves with the word of God.

Receive and Release Love

The familiar passage on love from 1 Corinthians, 13:4-8a is shown below, taken from The Passion Translation to offer new insight:

"Love is large and incredibly patient.
Love is gentle and consistently kind to all.
It refuses to be jealous when blessing comes to someone else.
Love does not brag about one's achievements nor inflate its own importance.
Love does not traffic in shame and disrespect, nor selfishly seek its own honor.
Love is not easily irritated or quick to take offense.
Love joyfully celebrates honesty and finds no delight in what is wrong.
Love is a safe place of shelter, for it never stops believing the best for others.
Love never takes failure as defeat for it never gives up."

Our representation of Jesus Christ should be one of love. Reading through these verses, it becomes clear that genuine love is impossible without God's help. The Bible tells us in 1 John 4:19, "We love, because He first loved us." It is

God's love within us that loves others well. "...God is love, and the one who abides in love abides in God, and God abides in him," (1 John 4:16). We receive love from the Father through Christ, then we return love back to Him and to others.

God loves us with His "agape" love, which means, "selfless, sacrificial, unconditional love. It is the highest of the four types of love in the Bible," (Learning Religions). This is the type of love God has for us and the love we can return to Him through Christ. Let us not love God based on what He does for us. The fact that Jesus died for us—granting eternal life and His abiding presence—is enough. Too often, unanswered prayers cause people to lose their devotion, suggesting our love for Him is conditional.

> "Teacher, which is the greatest commandment in the law?' And he said to him, 'You shall love the Lord your God, with all your heart, and with all your soul, and with all your mind.' This is the greatest and foremost commandment. The second is like it, 'you shall love your neighbor as yourself.'"
>
> Matthew 22: 37-39

Receive and Release Love

As we live in the Father's love, that love infuses our life. His love enables us to see others through its lens. Seeing people as He does—looking into their potential—we can speak into their purpose and destiny, calling those things forth.

There is a love deficit in our culture today. The broken and hurting are all around us. As people of God, we have the authority through Christ to free the oppressed. It is time to go beyond the four walls of the church and represent Jesus to a lost and dying world. We have the answers and solutions to the needs of humanity. God's love brings the freedom, healing, and restoration for which they are yearning; we carry this love. The harvest is ripe, which is why the time we are living in is so crucial. We were created, "...for such a time as this."[4] People need Jesus more than ever. Our love shines bright in a dark world.

Drawing closer to God is important if we want to be saturated in His love. People can feel the love of God radiating off a person. What we carry affects those around us. The more we love Him, the more we will love others. Let me share a few ways that have helped me increase my love connection with God:

- Worship
- Thanksgiving
- Adoration
- Singing
- Praise
- Soaking
- Listening
- Journaling
- Surrender
- Obedience
- Consistent quiet time

Our relationship with God is not simply about what God can do for us, it encompasses what we do in response to Him. When we make God's love a priority, we know His heart. Hearing His heart on matters enables us to pray for His purposes to come to pass, but it also allows us to respond in a heartfelt way to the needs of others.

The closer I get to the Lord, the more immersed in receiving and releasing His love, the stronger my desire is to know His heart. The temptation to sin grows dim. This is the way I am choosing to live, because I have noticed that staying in His will promotes love, peace, and joy. God's way of life is the high road, above all the chaos of the world.

As you and I develop our love relationship with Father God, we have something to give others. This love can even affect strangers on the street. It enables us to have mercy on the lost, knowing they don't understand what they are doing. In our day, with all the atmospheric rulers of darkness, the love we carry is a light for the world to see. May we shine brighter and brighter with the love of Christ.

Chapter Nuggets

- Love is the center of the Christian faith.
- Growing closer to God increases our understanding of His love.
- A love deficit allows counterfeits to take His place.
- We are sons or daughters, part of Father God's family, no longer orphans.
- Others will feel the love we carry.
- When we make God's love a priority, we will know His heart.
- As you and I develop our love relationship with the Lord, we have something to give others.

CHAPTER 10

Hear God's Heart

"Many of my people love their ministry more than me," the Lord told me in the middle of the night. This made me ponder, as I quickly thought of my own journey and wondered if this applied to me. The past couple of years, when my traveling and speaking ministry had nearly come to a halt, the Lord brought me closer to Himself. It was during this season that I wrote and published my first book, *Kingdom Benefits: Advantages of a New Life with Christ.*, I also spent my time interceding for our country.

I found myself in the prayer room at our church, dancing with banners, and engaging in prophetic intercession. This type of ministry goes way back for me. What I started to realize was this: I was experiencing the joy of the Lord while taking a walk, driving, or before falling asleep at night. It suddenly dawned on me that while we may think ministry is solely what pleases the Lord, that is not the case. He is pleased when we interact with Him. He is pleased when we acknowledge Him in all our daily activities. This led to the decompartmentalization I shared about in chapter five.

> "Whether then, you eat or drink, or whatever you do, do all to the glory of God."
>
> 1 Corinthians 10:31

In the first nine chapters, I wrote about ways to draw closer to God and how we can initiate this intimacy. Going forward, I will address the question, "Why bother?" Dutch Sheets, a popular teacher of the Word, says the following, "Our message will always in some way be deficient if it isn't motivated by the King's heart."

We can be credentialed in seminary, Bible school, ministry school, and more, with various renowned degrees. I am ordained with the Apostolic Network of Global Awakening. The world likes credentials. My husband is a retired family practice physician. His credentialing mattered a great deal to patients.

While biblical knowledge is important, there is more to our relationship with the Lord. The disciples of Jesus knew the Old Testament scriptures, but they also experienced kingdom life while Jesus walked with them. They participated in the works that Jesus did by preaching the gospel, healing the sick, and casting out demons. When the Holy Spirit came at Pentecost, He empowered and emboldened Christ followers to be witnesses to all the earth. They were baptized with tongues of fire and saw three thousand conversions in one day.

We can know *about* God; we can know all the stories and know His word. We can have head knowledge without the heart's participation. One of the reasons to draw closer to the Lord is to know His heart, which transcends the mind. Knowing His heart enables us to partner with Him, fully engaged. This means we live in a place of surrendering our will for His and actively seek to know Him.

Unfortunately, many believers look to the Lord to fulfill their own desires. We all have desires that we want satisfied. God in His goodness will satisfy our asking of things, but this cannot be the only time we seek Him. As we grow in Him, and as our love connection strengthens, our desires to be fully His come alive! Soon we start to understand that we live for Him and not He for us. Loving the Lord only because of what He can do for us will never be as fulfilling as tuning into His voice and partnering with what is in His heart. As we lean into Him, we can trust that God is a good Father Who has our best interests at heart.

How do we hear God's heart? We listen. Our maturity grows into, "What does God care about and how can I participate?" We move from this relationship being all about me, to a relationship being about listening to His voice and partnering in what He wants to accomplish. In my personal growth as a disciple, I experienced this taking place.

The Lord has plans for you and me, purposes to fulfill, and reasons we are alive at this time in history. What is in His heart for us to do? What are the plans He has for us? Are we willing to take the time to listen rather than just telling Him our troubles?

> "'For I know the plans that I have for you,' declares the Lord, 'plans for welfare and not for calamity to give you a future and a hope. Then you will call upon Me and come and pray to Me, and I will listen to you. You will seek me and find Me when you search for me with all your heart.'"
> Jeremiah 29:11-13

Jesus teaches us a desire of God's heart, and that is to love our neighbor. In Matthew 22:39b, He tells us that the second greatest commandment is this: "You shall love your neighbor as yourself." Who is our neighbor? Everyone but us. Our neighbor can signify family, friends, relatives, strangers, co-workers, even enemies. You and I often love conditionally, when people treat us right, when we share the same ideas, when we have the same likes and dislikes, when our personalities are agreeable, and so forth. We can love one another for looks, beliefs, job performance, what church we attend, or even what education we have. Natural love is all about conditions. Unless we have God's heart and compassion for people, what do we have to offer?

We would look no different than the world with performance-based love.

Jesus interacted with various kinds of people; tax collectors, Pharisees, Sadducees, religious rulers, outcasts, leppers, the deformed and maimed, demoniacs, fishermen, widows—there was no one He dismissed. The heart of Father God in Jesus Christ saw value in all mankind. We are all made in God's image. How could loving this way be possible for you and me, except by receiving His love for others?

Several years ago, I heard a story that I have never forgotten. A prophet shared about how the Lord spoke to Him regarding the sexual sin of his neighbor. The prophet was not particularly fond of his neighbor, so he was all ready to walk next door and share the word of the Lord. Halfway there, the Lord stopped him. "You are not ready to speak to your neighbor. Go home and fast for twenty-one days."

During the fast, the prophet encountered God's heart for his neighbor and wept. The fast ended and he went to his neighbor. While speaking the word of the Lord, he began weeping and the neighbor broke down as well. This exchange resulted in complete freedom for the neighbor. The Lord desires that we minister with His compassion and love saturating our hearts.

I heard another prophet share a story: The prophet was critiquing a particular actress. The Lord spoke and said, "I was going to use you to minister to this person, but because of your attitude, I will use another." The prophet repented, and God used him.

If our ministry is void of God's heart, and we only have knowledge, we can become judgmental, pointing out people's sin with our own pride. Romans 2 says, "Or do you think lightly of the riches of His kindness and tolerance and patience, not knowing that the kindness of God leads you to repentance?" We are not called to judge, but to provide people with the loving truth of God's word to set them free.

People know when you love them. They can feel it radiating from you. If you never invest the time in drawing near to God, you will miss hearing from Him regarding others. It will be those who commune with Him—those who linger in His presence—that will hear His heart for others and pray accordingly. Oftentimes, the Lord will bring someone to mind who needs prayer. This is beautiful.

Prophetic intercessors are those who hear what's on God's heart and intercede for His Kingdom to be released into that situation. A while back the Lord placed a movie star on my heart and said to pray for "his salvation." Within the next year, it came to pass, and he publicly acknowledged it.

Believers carry different intercessory assignments, and they know what assignment they have due to what's strongest in their heart. God has given armies of people an assignment to pray for our country. Those assigned, as I am one, can feel God's heart for our country. Prayer burdens involve the heart and prayers released from a burden may involve travail and weeping. God gives prayer burdens to bring His will to pass in the earth.

David's life is a prime example of one who knew the heart of God. "...I have found David, the son of Jesse, a man after My heart, who will do all My will," (Acts 13:22b). David's story is too extensive to go into detail, but he loved God. He was called out of shepherding in the field to be anointed king. His most famous story is the defeat of Goliath. David wrote at least seventy-five Psalms. He was a warrior and a worshipper. Although he made a couple bad decisions along the way, David ran back to the Lord, not away from Him.

"Draw near to God and He will draw near to you…" (James 4:8). Father God loves us passionately and longs for us to know Him intimately. Before sin entered the world in the Garden of Eden, God walked in close relationship with Adam and Eve. The way God knew His children in the garden, prior to the fall, is the way we can know Him now. This knowing is more than head knowledge; it reaches into the depths of our hearts and immerses us in His glorious love.

As we begin to know God's heart, His desires and ours will coincide. A prime example is my short-term missionary work. This is on God's heart for me as well as in my heart to do. If you have a talent as an artist, then God also desires in His heart that you develop your talent. God's heart for us is not contrary to the gifts He has given us.

God is creative and so are we. Many of my creative ideas are from Him. In fact, any time I have an idea I ponder if He originated it. The closer we become to God, the more our ideas and thoughts line up with His, bearing much fruit. Our hearts become intertwined in this beautiful place of intimacy.

Chapter Nuggets

- "Many of my people love their ministry more than Me."
- "Our message will always in some way be deficient if it isn't motivated by the King's heart." – Dutch Sheets.
- There is more to experience than gaining credentials.
- Knowing God's heart enables us to partner with Him fully.
- As we draw near to God, we will hear His voice on that for which He wants us to pray.
- What is in His heart and ours will coincide.
- Knowing God intimately reaches into the depths of our hearts and immerses us in His glorious love.

CLOSER

CHAPTER 11

Withstand Culture

I found myself catching my breath and gasping over the pandemic issues: uprising of crime, riots, looting, whistleblowers fighting for their lives, kids changing genders, and the complete sabotage of the United States. I could sense all the anger within this country, and I wanted to fight the people responsible.

The Holy Spirit has spoken to me about being watchful over how much news I view. As an intercessor for America, I pray in response to the news. I call forth the purposes of God for this nation. I am a watchwoman sending forth the angels of God to fulfill His plans.

Spiritual warfare is blatantly obvious in this hour. Voices yell from every corner, urging us to join in the parade of accepting whatever anyone feels like doing. Sin is no longer hidden in the closet; it is marched down our streets for all to see. Those who are on the fence between God and the world risk falling off on the wrong side.

"Watch over your heart with all diligence, for from it flow the springs of life."

Proverbs 4:23

Christian leaders, or any believer of Christ, risk falling away if they become too busy and neglect watching over their hearts. Ministry does not take the place of quiet time. Any service for the Lord is secondary to our time of prayer. Your spiritual resolve comes from internal strength that is fortified by the Holy Spirit.

"...because the kingdom of God is within you."
Luke 17:21 NIV

The stronger our personal relationship is with the Lord, the less tempted we are to join in with the plans of darkness. The abiding presence of the Holy Spirit helps us live a holy life devoted to God, even when chaos abounds. 1 John 4:4 says it all:

"Greater is He who is in you, than he who is in the world." Christ in us is a more powerful force than the darkness in the world; however, we must protect our hearts and stay watchful.

> "But the fruit of the Spirit is love, joy, peace, patience, kindness, goodness, faithfulness, gentleness, self-control; against such things there is no law."
>
> Galatians 5:22

The fruit of the Spirit continues to mature within us throughout our spiritual journey. These attributes of a Christlike nature are internal, yet they regulate our external world. Where there is anger and fear in the atmosphere, we are called to love. Where there is oppression, we can release joy. Where there is anxiety, we can release peace. We represent the kingdom of Heaven by responding to situations with the character of Christ. The Holy Spirit has made much progress in my life in these areas, but He is still working. As a "do-it-now kind of gal, patience is hard.

Recently, I went on a mission's trip to Rwanda, Africa. The first flight was delayed six hours, which meant I missed the second flight. Eighteen people found themselves stuck in Nigeria's airport. It was very hot with no place to sit, the immigration department took all our passports, and there was no immediate solution. The cascade of missed flights led to more days of delay and finally, after four days, my friend and I arrived in Kigali, Rwanda. Many people were angry. This was a test of faith. Would I depend on God's grace and trust Him for peace during chaos? It was tempting to grumble and complain, and I did so for a bit. But through prayer, God helped me stay in peace.

My dependency was on my inner world, where the Kingdom of God reigns. The fruit of the Spirit is our holding power during times of uncertainty. It is our stability, our immovable stance when trouble comes. I had no control over this situation as we were being herded about by the immigration department. I had peace, I had patience, I had a couple jokes, and I knew God was with me. I was incredibly grateful the Lord helped me through.

The first time you go into the gym, your ability to lift weights and do certain moves with the bar will be at a beginner's level. The more you work out your muscles, the stronger you become. It is the same way with Kingdom principles. The more you feed your spirit man with the word, prayer, worship, praise, and thanksgiving, the stronger He becomes. As you allow time to commune with God, the more His reign in your life becomes a force that is immovable, steadfast, and not giving into worldly culture.

In Matthew 22:37, Jesus reminds us: "You shall love the Lord your God with all your heart, and with all your soul, and with all your mind." Our inner world navigates our external world. If the Lord reigns in our heart—if He is our first love—then all the fears, trials, adversities, losses, and disappointments that we face will be navigated with Him.

"For our struggle is not against flesh and blood, but against the rulers, against the powers, against the world forces of this darkness, against the spiritual forces of wickedness in the heavenly places." Ephesians 6:12.

God has given us weapons, the armor of God, to stand firm and withstand the schemes of the devil. These are valuable tools to use as needed. The enemy can be relentless in His attacks, but we have the weaponry to stand firm and overtake

Him. We have the helmet of salvation, sword of the Spirit, shield of faith, breastplate of righteousness, loins of truth, and feet covered in the gospel of peace. We are called to stay alert and pray.

Towns, cities, states, and nations all have physical as well as spiritual climates. For example, I can recall feeling evil spirits in Disney World's Haunted Mansion. I remember feeling fear in hospitals. I have felt doom and gloom in nursing homes. Why do people not want to play in graveyards? We have the authority through Christ to speak in any climate and release the Kingdom.

We are equipped to withstand anything the world throws at us. Christ in us, the Holy Spirit, and the authority given to believers over the power of the enemy sets us up for victory. We are here to impact the world for the Kingdom of God. Our internal navigation system must triumph over the darkness everywhere we go. We represent Christ as the light of the world. We are the salt of the earth. Our relationship with God should be so close that when we walk into scary places, we release His love and peace.

> "For God has not given us a spirit of fear, but of power, love and a sound mind."
> 2 Timothy 1:7 KJV

I sense the Lord wanting His people to draw closer to Him so that they can withstand the pressure of culture. Churches are compromising the Word instead of modeling righteous conduct. Righteousness has not changed its definition; right standing with God means living according to His word and His ways. This is not out of performance or duty, but a love relationship, a partnership, and a desire to live life together as one. As Paul puts it in Colossians 1;27, "...Christ in you, the hope of glory." We have the indwelling Holy Spirit to help us live surrendered, not enticed by the world, but fully devoted to Christ Jesus.

Chapter Nuggets

- Be watchful over how much news you view. It impacts your heart.
- The stronger your personal relationship is, the less you give in to temptation.
- The fruit of the Spirit is developed over time.
- The Kingdom of God is an internal kingdom.
- The more we feed our spirit, the easier overcoming temptation becomes.
- Through Christ, our spiritual strength can withstand the worldly climate.
- We should be so aware of Christ in us, that when we walk into scary places, we release the love and peace of God.

CHAPTER 12

Advance the Kingdom

I am gripped with the assignment to speak to people in the streets with an encouraging word. One day my friend and I were in a mall parking lot ready to go inside. I noticed a couple getting out of their truck and felt the nudge of the Holy Spirit to speak to them. I had heart-shaped lollipops in my hand—a reminder of God's love. As I introduced myself, handing them a lollipop and a scripture card, they choked up. They said they recently lost their daughter, and this was assurance of God being with them. We prayed and exchanged hugs.

Serving the Lord can have challenges from society's backlash. This is not a season to hide and wait until a more opportune time. The Lord needs all His people to demonstrate the Kingdom to the world, reaping the harvest and making disciples. The church needs a revelation that God's voice can influence culture. The people of God have separated themselves from the world instead of following Jesus' call to go into the world. Mark 16:15 says, "Go into all the world and preach the gospel to all creation."

As blood bought citizens of Heaven, we have the same authority as Jesus. Being His disciples, we can do the works He did. Jesus tells us in John 14:12, "Truly, truly, I say to you, he who believes in Me, the works that I do, he will do also; and greater works than these he will do; because I go to the Father." The more we pray for people, the more people will encounter the love and power of God. Our necessity to demonstrate the kingdom is not up for debate.

I have a tee shirt which says, "Kingdom Carrier." I am eagerly anticipating the day when miracles will become commonplace outside the four walls of the church. A powerful move of God has already begun, and we can participate as we live aware of His voice guiding us. Whether in the marketplace, workplace, schools, campus, or Hollywood studio, we shall see great demonstrations of God's love and power touching people.

We are called to "destroy the works of the devil" as Jesus did. 1 John 3:8 says, "...the one who practices sin is of the devil; for the devil has sinned from the beginning. The Son of God appeared for this purpose, to destroy the works of the devil." The closer we are to God, the more we live ready to dismantle the works of the enemy by delivering the oppressed, healing the sick, and saving the lost. We know whose we are and the authority we carry.

It is important for you and me to hear God's strategy for anything He asks of us. Joshua had an interesting assignment from the Lord regarding how to overcome Jericho.

"You shall march around the city, all the men of war circling the city once. You shall do so for six days. Also, seven priests shall carry seven rams' horns before the ark; then on the seventh day you shall march around the city seven times, and the priests shall blow the trumpets. It shall be that when they make a long blast with the ram's horn, and when you hear the sound of the trumpet, all the people shall shout with a great shout; and the wall of the city will fall down flat, and the people will go up every man straight ahead."

Joshua 6:4-5

This story is a great testimony as to why we need to hear from the Lord. There may be a different route of navigation than what we have done in the past. I have noticed God likes to switch things up. I raise funds for travel, and He continuously gives me various ways to ask for donations. When the Lord gives us direction, He provides grace to fulfill the task as we respond in obedience. If we hear His plan, then adopt our own ideas to carry it out, we won't bear any fruit.

When it comes to comparing our God-given assignments to others', picture a fishing net. There are knots all over the net, holding it together. If one knot is severed, a hole appears. Which knot is more important? None of them. They all have a part in the construction of the net. Just like you and I in the kingdom. We all have a part to play. The baby toe is part of the body and so is the eye. All parts are important. God has not called everyone to be platform preachers, but all are called to impact society. No matter what your vocation is, God has a plan to release His kingdom through you.

Keep your ears and eyes open to see what God is doing in your midst. How can we bring the Lord into our workplaces? Into the lives of those around us? Do we notice opportunities to pray for others? To encourage them? Can we live in love and not offense? Are we quick to forgive? Do we carry His peace to a level at which we can release it in times of stress or hardship?

I take time for mini trips into the marketplace. My friend and I hand out books, scripture cards, chocolate hugs and kisses, and lollipops for kids. We tell people, "We are prayer walking and handing out hugs and kisses." Then we show them our chocolate. It immediately breaks down their defenses and opens the door for conversation. Many receive prayer and thank us for what we are doing.

The prophetic gift is powerful in the streets. People are curious to hear from the Lord. I ask their permission to share first, and after giving a word, I get their feedback. God recently gave me a word of knowledge—specific insight regarding a person He wants me to reach. He told me to pray for a man in a red shirt regarding a financial situation. I was ministering at a prayer tent that day. I found the man, and he explained that he was being sued over inheritance that was rightfully his. God wanted to bring a solution and resolve the issue. It was very encouraging to the man.

> "Then He said to His disciples, 'The harvest is plentiful, but the workers are few. Therefore, beseech the Lord of the harvest to send out workers into His harvest.'"
>
> Matthew 9:37-38

God will use anyone who is willing and yielded. There are so many ways to be effective in advancing the kingdom. There is no one-size-fits-all method. Sharing testimonies, offering to pray for people, releasing encouraging words, however you feel led to display Jesus, works.

In this season, I believe God is promoting His people to higher levels, giving us His perspective and leading us into greater assignments. My recent trip to Rwanda saw greater Holy Spirit activity than ever, with many salvations and healings. May we be conduits of the love and power of Jesus, resulting in salvations, healings, and miracles wherever we go. Let us bring Heaven to earth, advancing the Kingdom and making disciples of all nations.

Chapter Nuggets

- We are called to be about Father God's business.
- Serving the Lord in our present day has backlash from society.
- We have been given authority over the enemy's power in Jesus' name.
- We all have a part to play in influencing the world for Christ.
- Know God's strategy of how to advance His kingdom.
- There is no one-size-fits-all method.
- May we be conduits of the love and power of Jesus.

CHAPTER 13

Represent Jesus

I led a team of ten people from my church to Puerto Rico on a mission's trip. On the itinerary was a service project to be announced when we got there. I am all about ministry on trips, so building, painting, and that sort of thing belongs to others on the team. We found out we would be cleaning a man's home which he inherited from his mother who had passed away. Her stuff was still in it, and he was overwhelmed. Our directors anticipated an eight-hour project for the thirteen helpers.

We prayed, the team chose their rooms to clean, and we went to work. There was grease all over the stove and wall beside it. There were cobwebs throughout, and all the blinds were dirty. There was grime, dirt, and layers of clutter to be sorted and thrown away. There was mold coating the sidewalk. There were overgrown weeds and broken outdoor furniture. The team set up a boom box with worship music. After three-and-a-half hours of hard work and sweat, we were done. The house was clean, scrubbed inside and out. The mold was gone. We deodorized and made everything smell fresh. The owner was so blessed, he wept. The team just gushed over God's help to do this project—an opportunity that no one had originally wanted. This was a marked event from our trip that everyone will remember—the day Jesus helped us show kindness and clean a man's home.

I share this story and receive such a blessing in my heart every time I think about it, because this man then came to a special church service on a Tuesday night. He was thrilled above and beyond! When it comes to representing Christ, there are multiple ways to be kind, helpful, generous, show compassion to people, and help meet their needs.

It is an awesome privilege and honor we have, to be Christ's representatives. To represent Him, we need to be like Him. This means receiving freedom from our bad habits and choosing to live God's way. We are all at different places in our journey. He provides ongoing revelation to show us what needs changed in our walk, and the more we yield our life to His, the more He brings about those changes. Mentors are a godsend for their prayers and guidance helping us grow.

The process of transformation begins the day of salvation. 2 Corinthians 5:17 tells us: "Therefore, if anyone is in Christ, he is a new creation; the old has gone, the new has come." Our new-life training and equipping to be Christlike are the makings of a disciple: one who is called to be like their teacher.

> "And do not be conformed to this world, but be transformed by the renewing of your mind, so that you may prove what the will of God is, that which is good and acceptable and perfect."
>
> Romans 12:2

Joining the Kingdom results in salvation for your spirit. Your mind and soul, however, undergo a transformation in learning how to live according to the word of God. The more we surrender our fleshly ways to Jesus, the more He can change us into His image. Paul writes in Galatians 2:20, "I have been crucified with Christ; and it is no longer I who live, but Christ lives in me; and the life which I now live in the flesh I live by faith in the Son of God, who loved me and gave Himself up for me."

The rule and reign of the Kingdom should inhabit every sphere of our life. We don't choose salvation, then live like the world. Our spirit man gets saved, then our mind and body go through a renewal—a transformational process. Our thinking, speaking and activities are now for God's glory and pleasure. As we change, from caterpillar to butterfly, others will notice our change.

Our representation of Jesus is for the world to see Him, but first, our personal relationship must be developed in the secret place. How we conduct ourselves—how we respond to situations and circumstances—will manifest Jesus or the world, we choose. If we curse the troublemakers, that is an inferior representation. The beauty of living like Christ is that He enables us, by His grace, to respond in the love of God.

Give yourself grace on this journey of becoming like Christ. Some issues may dissolve overnight, and some may take time. The closer you are to Him, the more you can spot trouble in your heart or mind. A consistent prayer I have is for God to plow the soil of my heart and pluck out any weeds.

How do we represent Christ? What do others see in our words and actions? Do we look like the world? Do people enjoy being around us? Jesus had huge crowds following Him. As His reputation for multiplying food, healing, and deliverance spread, so the crowds grew.

"You know of Jesus of Nazareth, how God anointed Him with the Holy Spirit and with power, and how He went about doing good and healing all who were oppressed by the devil, for God was with Him."

Acts 10:38

You and I have the same Holy Spirit Jesus did. We can also pray for the sick and see them recover. The miracles of Christ are still relevant today as the Bible tells us in Hebrews 13:8 that, "Jesus Christ is the same yesterday, today, and forever." We preach the gospel by sharing His word and testimonies of His goodness.

During my years ministering in Rio de Janeiro, I prayed for many people and saw them get touched by the Holy Spirit. Pain left, back issues fled, and many received healing in their hearts as they wept and fell to the ground. Participating in doing the works that Jesus did brings me great delight and Him, glory. Don't give up this effort. People need Jesus and they need to know He is real. His power demonstrates this.

As we respond to people with love and kindness, seeing them through the eyes of our Creator, believing they have value besides their sinful behavior, it changes lives. Rather than being quick to judge, condemn, or criticize, we take time to speak words that encourage. As James 1:19-20 puts it, "But everyone must be quick to hear, slow to speak and slow to anger; for the anger of man does not achieve the righteousness of God."

"Let no unwholesome word proceed from your mouth, but only such a word as is good for edification according to the need of the moment, so that it will give grace to those that hear. Do not grieve the Holy Spirit of God, by whom you were sealed for the day of redemption. Let all bitterness and wrath and anger and clamor and slander be put away from you, along with all malice. Be kind to one another, tender-hearted, forgiving each other, just as God in Christ has also forgiven you."

Ephesians 4:29-32

Another way we represent Jesus is through our words. The way you and I speak to one another will either be godly or ungodly. Being confrontational, arrogant, and doing all the talking is a direct turn off to the listener. In my family, when the kids were growing up, there were several things we did not allow our kids to say to one another or their friends. This list included words such as "stupid," "jerk," "dumb," "idiot," and "retarded.' We wanted to teach them to honor and value people.

How well do we represent Jesus with our words? Are we positive? Encouraging? Comforting? Or are we always complaining, grumbling, and criticizing? After understanding the power of words—that they bless and curse—I want my words to bring life, healing, and wholeness. God can back up those words. Words of destruction, on the other hand, enlist the enemy's power to harm.

Joy is a great representation of Christ. How great it is to have joy! People need joy because, "„,the joy of the Lord is your strength," (Nehemiah 8:10b).

According to research by Charles and Frances Hunter in *Laugh Yourself Healthy*,[5] here is the anatomy of a laugh:

- Your heart and lungs are stimulated.
- Your heart beats faster and your blood pressure rises temporarily.
- You breathe deeper and oxygenate more blood. Your body releases endorphins—your own natural painkillers—and you produce more immune cells.
- You burn seventy-eight times as many calories as you would in a resting state.
- Your diaphragm, facial muscles, and internal organs all get bounced around in what is sometimes called, "internal jogging."

"After you've laughed, your muscles and arteries relax. That's great for easing pain. Also, your blood pressure lowers, and your pulse drops below normal. Some researchers think all this aids digestion."

I ministered in nursing homes and the Lord would always give me joy for the people. It blesses my heart tremendously to see people touched with joy: those who are in wheelchairs, in a hospital bed, or stricken with fear. The joy of the Lord brings breakthrough in the spirit.

Romans 14:17 explains, "...for the kingdom of God is not eating and drinking, but righteousness, and peace and joy in the Holy Spirit." Peace is an incredible force. With all the turbulence in the world—with all the chaotic evil—peace is one thing believers do not want to lose. Turn aside from what promotes upset and decree the word of the Lord. Walk by faith. "The steadfast of mind You will keep in perfect peace, because he trusts in You," Isaiah 26:3. Peace is something we carry and can release. Jesus is the "Prince of Peace," as stated in Isaiah 9:6. I guard this daily in my life.

Drawing closer to the Lord will help us grow in the likeness of Christ. This likeness enables us to represent Him well on the earth. People are looking at our lives and determining if our

Christianity means anything. How has it helped us? Does our lifestyle entice them to choose Jesus? It should. We walk in the supernatural love and power of God every day. We are their opportunity to experience Christ.

> 1 John 4:17 "...because as He is, so also are we in this world."

Representing Jesus is an ongoing process. It is purposeful and intentional to live in agreement with the Kingdom. Knowing what the word of God says, coupled with doing what the word says, will bear much fruit. It is the pursuit of righteousness. People notice. They notice how you treat them, if you love them, and if you honor the word of the Lord. We can't live this way out of self-effort. This is a life of faith through God's grace.

Chapter Nuggets

- Transformation begins the day of salvation.
- Our representation of Christ is for others to see Him in us, but first our personal relationship must be developed in the secret place.
- Live without offense and choose love.
- Our words activate the kingdom of Heaven or darkness.
- The joy of the Lord is not dependent on external circumstances.
- Representing Jesus is an ongoing process.
- We walk in the supernatural love and power of God every day.

CLOSER

CHAPTER 14

Holy Spirit Operations

Growing up in the Lutheran church, my first Holy Spirit experience came after leaving my hometown. While my husband attended medical school, I met some on-fire believers, and they asked me if I spoke in tongues. My response: "What's that?" I don't recall their explanation enticing me to receive this gift. In fact, when one of my new friends showed up at my house telling me the Lord told her to pray for me to have this, I was immediately scared. Timidly I said, "Okay." She proceeded to pray, rebuked fear, and then prayed for me to receive. When she finished, I said, "I think I got this, but you go home so I can practice alone." She left and for the next hour I blurted out this Holy Spirit language and joy overflowed my heart.

My life was forever changed. No longer did I consider going to church simply a requirement for Heaven's gates. No longer was prayer a must, but it became a want to. I got excited about Jesus in a whole new way. It would be another fourteen years before we ventured into a non-denominational church and knew this was what the Lord wanted for my family.

I don't know about you, but for me, I need adventure in my life. I need excitement surrounding my spiritual journey. Considering God created the heavens and the earth, why ever doubt that God is exciting? Loves adventure? Loves creating? We are made in His image. It is exciting to read through the Bible at all the exploits ordinary people accomplished through the power of God.

Jesus tells his disciples in Acts 1:8, "But you shall receive power when the Holy Spirit has come upon you; and you shall be My witnesses both in Jerusalem, and in all Judea and Samaria, and even to the remotest part of the earth." The

Holy Spirit showed up. "And there appeared to them tongues as of fire, distributing themselves, and they rested on each one of them. And they were all filled with the Holy Spirit, and began to speak with other tongues, as the Spirit was giving them utterance." Acts 3,4. They began speaking in languages they did not know, because the Holy Spirit was praying through them. The crowd marveled when they heard their native languages coming from the mouths of these people. It was miraculous.

What the disciples experienced is called the baptism of the Holy Spirit. The Holy Spirit came upon those in the upper room, empowering them to be witnesses and demonstrate the gospel. My spiritual life changed dramatically when I was baptized in the Holy Spirit with the evidence of speaking in tongues. I felt so much closer to Jesus. My passion for Him and my devotion to Him increased tremendously.

The baptism of the Holy Spirit may result in the gift of tongues, or it may not. Encounters with the Holy Spirit take on many manifestations: some people fall under the power, some weep, shake, laugh, feel heat, electricity, and more.

When we receive the Holy Spirit at salvation, He comes as an abiding presence, to bring about our new life and begin transforming us into Christ's image. The Holy Spirit encountering us, as on the day of Pentecost, is for ministering unto others.

> "After being baptized, Jesus came up immediately from the water; behold, the heavens were opened, and He saw the Spirit of God descending as a dove and lighting on Him..."
>
> Matthew 3:16

The Holy Spirit descended and remained upon Jesus. The Bible tells us in 1 John 4:17, "...as He is, so also are we in this world." Jesus is our role-model for life. If His ministry was full of the Holy Spirit, we can rest assured that the activity of the Holy Spirit is for our ministry too.

I have mentioned in prior chapters about the fruit of the Spirit and how this fruit is grown and developed throughout our journey. This is one role of the Holy Spirit but not the only one. Another role He plays in our life is providing the gifts of the Spirit, which are listed in 1 Corinthians 12:8-10:

- <u>Word of Wisdom</u>-God showing you how to proceed, His way.
- <u>Word of Knowledge</u>-Present or past information about a person that God reveals.
- <u>Prophecy</u>-A word of encouragement, exhortation, or comfort.
- <u>Faith</u>-Belief for miracles with no doubt, unbelief, or fear.
- <u>Healing</u>-Miracle gift in which God restores people's health through you.
- <u>Miracles</u>-When you pray, God performs instantaneous restoration.
- <u>Tongues</u>-Holy Spirit language.
- <u>Interpretation of Tongues</u>-When a word is spoken in tongues that is intended for an individual or group to receive, God gives you the interpretation of what is said so you can translate.
- <u>Distinguishing of Spirits</u>-Recognizing if a voice is of the flesh, devil, or God.

These gifts are deposited in seed form when we receive the Holy Spirit at salvation. Gifts can also be magnified and stirred up during times of impartation from others who operate in them. The more we practice our gifts, the stronger they become, and we see which ones bear the most fruit. Speaking in tongues is the one gift that edifies and encourages us; however, this gift may also be utilized in a church service to bring encouragement to the body. All the others are a demonstration of God's revelation and power.

This is a very exciting way to partner with the Lord. We have the equipment and the user manual to operate in the supernatural to meet the needs of our ailing society. As Christ followers, we carry within us supernatural power that enables us to do the works that Jesus did.

It is vital to keep in mind that the gifts operate by the Holy Spirit, and we cannot become prideful or boastful in ourselves. It is not our power—we have none—it is all God's power flowing through us by the Holy Spirit. A second important note, the gift of God can operate through one who is in hidden sin. We see leaders being exposed, and they are still gifted. Judas was sent out with all the other disciples to preach the word and pray for healing and deliverance.

Gifts are powerful, but they should not exclude or override our obedience to the Lord in personal areas of humility, righteousness, and trust. I believe that when people become overly busy serving the Lord, neglecting their quiet time, they become open to temptation.

Jesus ministered out of love and compassion, and so should we. 1 Corinthians 13:2 explains the importance of this quite nicely: "If I have the gift of prophecy and know all mysteries and all knowledge; and if I have all faith, so as to remove mountains, but do not have love, I am nothing," Love is our motivator for using our gifts. Because we love people, we want to see their lives healed and prospering. God's desires for people become our desires for them. Our heart-to-heart connection with God directly influences how we see and treat people.

"I will ask the Father, and He will give you another Helper, that He may be with you forever; that is the Spirit of truth, whom the world cannot receive, because it does not see Him or know Him, but you know Him because He abides with you and will be in you." John 14:16-17.

Jesus is calling the Holy Spirit a Helper and Spirit of truth. The Holy Spirit helps us in our discipleship process. The Holy Spirit will bring conviction when we err on the side of sin. He will help us align with the truth of God's word when we begin to stray. The Holy Spirit is there to empower us to live righteously. While we do not pray to the Holy Spirit, He helps us use His gifts to manifest the power of God and show God's love to the world around us.

Randy Clark, President of Global Awakening, teaches that hunger is the component for encounters with the Holy Spirit. There are sovereign encounters as well, and one of those examples is Paul. He never asked for his encounter on the road to Damascus, but it changed his life forever. Divine encounters often show up in corporate settings where the Holy Spirit is moving powerfully. They can bring increased anointing for ministry, deliverance, healing, fire, or renewal and refreshing. I have had many divine encounters over the course of my Jesus journey. They have fueled my passion for Christ.

> "But I tell you the truth, it is to your advantage that I go away; for if I do not go away, the Helper will not come to you; but if I go, I will send Him to you. And He, when He comes, will convict the world concerning sin and righteousness and judgment..." John 16:7-8

Conviction helps keep us in divine alignment with God. Anything outside of His truth triggers a sense of wrongdoing in the heart. This can be felt by believers and non-believers. It's a knowing of wrongdoing—a recognition of the sinful nature. Conviction can come when we have ungodly thoughts, speak harmful words, or engage in immoral deeds. This is a great help in keeping us from sin. Hebrews 12:10b tells us that, "...He disciplines us for our good, so that we may share in His holiness." The Holy Spirit is the Spirit of truth, and the truth of God's word sets us free.

I have no desire to engage with darkness and interfere with the fullness of God's Kingdom manifesting in me. This is a journey, not an instantaneous makeover. The closer you live to the Lord, the more areas of life you have surrendered to Him, the easier it is to recognize when something is amiss. He is patient with us and forgiving as we repent. Any struggles you may have, trust God for deliverance. Freedom, healing, and more are available to you through the power of the Holy Spirit. God is good, and His goodness is available to you today.

Chapter Nuggets

- The Holy Spirit is an abiding presence upon salvation.
- Manifestations are the result of the Holy Spirit coming upon people.
- Jesus received the Holy Spirit at His baptism.
- The gifts function solely by the Holy Spirit and not from our own ability.
- The Holy Spirit helps us in our discipleship process. Jesus ministered out of love and compassion and so should we.
- The Holy Spirit convicts us of sin, setting us free after we repent.

CHAPTER 15

Closer

Drawing closer to God in this hour is His call to all of us. There is always more and lest we grow stagnant, keeping this in mind is essential. The worldly voices clamoring for our attention and distracting our focus surround us. It is intentional that we turn aside and hear what the Lord is saying to us.

> "The angel of the Lord appeared to him in a blazing fire from the midst of a bush; and he looked, and behold, the bush was burning with fire, yet the bush was not consumed. So Moses said, 'I must turn aside now and see this marvelous sight, why the bush in not burned up.'"
> Exodus 3:2-3

God initiated this burning bush encounter, but Moses had to respond to it. The encounter was profound as Moses heard the audible voice of God give direction. This massive assignment required this type of prominent communication, leaving no doubt.

It is not God's primary method in this new covenant day, to speak to His people through a burning bush, or other supernatural phenomena, although He can. His desire is that our ears would be attuned to hearing Him like Jesus did. "For I did not speak on my own initiative, but the Father Himself who sent Me, has given me a commandment as to what to say and what to speak. " John 12:49. My experience in drawing closer to God, enables me to hear clearer, and stay tuned in.

The development in our quiet time of hearing God's voice, benefits us throughout our day. He may speak to us to pray for someone needing healing, comfort, to share an encouraging word, or even to present the gospel. The point is, are we ready to obey when He speaks? Are we close enough to hear Him, discerning His voice, and know His heart in the matter?

Closer

The closer we are to the Lord, the more revelation we receive. Revelation is simply inspired knowledge. Scriptures, hearing God's voice, preaching, dreams, nature, books, and prophecy, are some of the ways that revelation comes. He can also speak through movies, songs, TV, and other secular media. Not only do we receive revelation, but we also learn who we are in Christ, and how to conduct ourselves as disciples in the earth.

Contrary to the ways of the world, is the kingdom lifestyle. The modes of operation are vastly different. "The thief comes only to steal and kill and destroy; I came that they may have life and have it abundantly." John 10:10. Our representation of the kingdom will be directly impacted by the amount of time we give unto the Lord to transform us. This requires us to pray, study His word, and surrender our ways to His.

The strength to overcome temptation also comes from the place of intimacy and surrender. David strengthened Himself in the Lord, and we must also. Drawing close to Him on a regular basis will fortify us in times of adversity or even persecution. "Be of sober spirit, your adversary, the devil, prowls around like a roaring lion, seeking someone to devour." 1 Peter. 5:8. Jesus overcame the devil, and so can we!

I went through a season of being still. The analogy was that of a vehicle parked in a mechanic's shop. I gave God permission to tune-up or overhaul my heart, whatever He desired. Out of this season came an identity alignment, with new revelation on my value as a daughter of the Most High God, a heavenly promotion. No longer could the enemy tempt me to think I was "less than."

As I write this final chapter, I can feel the pull in my heart. "Draw near to God, and He will draw near to you." "Humble yourselves in the presence of the Lord, and He will exalt you." James 4: 8, 10. There is much yet to be accomplished, but all our assignments should be surrounded by the powerful love of God. This agape, unconditional love of our Father increases as we come into the secret place to commune with Him.

The three- fold purpose of drawing closer is to God is 1) Knowing the Godhead. 2) Identity and personal transformation, and 3) sharing the good news with the demonstration of the kingdom.

The love of the Father, cultivated in intimacy, is the foundation for all the gifts of the Holy Spirit. May Jesus be made known by you and me receiving all glory and honor. Let us draw closer, receiving fresh revelation, releasing heaven on earth.

Blessings.

Chapter Nuggets

- Drawing closer to God in this hour is His call to all of us.
- God initiated the burning bush encounter, but Moses had to respond to it.
- The development in our quiet time of hearing God's voice, benefits us throughout our day.
- The closer we are to the Lord, the more revelation we receive.
- Our representation of the Kingdom will be directly impacted by the amount of time we give to the Lord to transform us.
- The threefold purpose of drawing closer is, 1) Knowing the Godhead 2) Identity and personal transformation and 3) The sharing of the good news and demonstration of the Kingdom.

Salvation

If you feel led to receive Jesus into your heart today, below is a prayer for salvation.

Dear God,

Today I confess Jesus Christ as my personal Savior and Lord of my life. I invite you Jesus, into my heart and surrender my life for Yours. I believe You carried my sin to the cross, were crucified, dead, and buried. You rose again granting me forgiveness and new life. I choose this day to follow you, to walk in Your ways, and to seek first Your kingdom. In Jesus' name I pray, amen.

Congratulations! You have just made the most important decision of your life. If you prayed this prayer, please contact me or tell another Christian as you begin your new journey with Jesus.

Notes

1. "The Consequences of Fatherlessness." *National Center for Fathering*, fathers.com/the-consequences-of-fatherlessness/.

2. "Obedience." *Holman Illustrated Bible Dictionary*, Holman Bible Publishers, 2003, p. 1206.

3. Walton, Owen. "Greek and Hebrew Words for Worship." *From These Shores*, 7 Oct. 2020, fromtheseshores.com/greek-hebrew-words-worship/.

4. Esther 4:14b, *New American Standard Bible 1995*.

5. Hunter, Charles, and Frances Hunter. *Laugh Yourself Healthy*. Christian Life, 2008, p. IX.

About the Author

Diane Burke is the founder of Diane Burke Ministries. She has completed Rhema Bible school instructional courses and is ordained as an Itinerant Minister through the Apostolic Network of Global Awakening in Mechanicsburg, Pennsylvania.

Diane is a prophetic voice with a passion to see people encounter the love and power of the Holy Spirit, bringing transformation. She has served in various roles in the local church and community: preacher, discipleship teacher, women's ministry leader, prayer watch coordinator, outreach leader, church staff and more. She is now traveling and speaking internationally.

Diane and Paul have four grown children, three married along with eight grandchildren. They currently reside in York Haven, Pennsylvania.

Connect with Diane Burke Ministries Online

Website: www.DianeBurkeMinistries.com

Email: DBM@DianeBurkeMinistries.com

Facebook: www.Facebook.com/dbmARISE

More Books from Diane Burke

Kingdom Benefits:
Advantages of a New Life with Christ

Available on Amazon!

www.ingramcontent.com/pod-product-compliance
Lightning Source LLC
Chambersburg PA
CBHW060534100426
42743CB00009B/1526